D0455242

THE PATHS TO
SOCIAL DEVIANCE AND CONFORMITY

A Model of the Process

Alvin Rudoff

HM
291
R752
1991

The Edwin Mellen Press
Lewiston/Queenston/Lampeter

RASMUSON LIBRARY
UNIVERSITY OF ALASKA-FAIRBANKS
Withdrawn
Surplus/Duplicate

Library of Congress Cataloging-in-Publication Data

Rudoff, Alvin.
   The paths to social deviance and conformity : a model of the
process / Alvin Rudoff.
   p.   cm.
   Includes bibliographical references and index.
   ISBN 0-7734-9438-3
   1. Deviant behavior--Mathematical models. 2. Conformity-
-Mathematical models. I. Title.
HM291.R752   1992
302.5'42--dc20   91-39309
                                                                CIP

A CIP catalog record for this book
is available from the British Library.

Copyright © 1991 Alvin Rudoff.

All rights reserved. For information contact

The Edwin Mellen Press   The Edwin Mellen Press
        Box 450   Box 67
Lewiston, New York   Queenston, Ontario
   USA 14092   CANADA L0S 1L0

Edwin Mellen Press, Ltd.
Lampeter, Dyfed, Wales
UNITED KINGDOM SA48 7DY

Printed in the United States of America

For Belle

Table of Contents

PREFACE

There is a Cornucopia of information about deviance. A good deal of it is popularized or journalistic. Some is ideological or speculative. But a sufficient amount is mature and scholarly covering theory and research as well as practice and experience. This rich legacy strives for science with theory and empirical evidence. Though not always attained, the results have developed a body of knowledge conducive to accurate theorizing and directions for further research.

Theories of deviance are relatively new. Theories of specific types of deviance (e.g. suicide, crime and mental illness) were the precursors of deviance theory. Both kinds were criticized, especially for the lack of empirical content and/or their limitations. Yet in retrospect, the level of sophistication and abstraction increased. In short, each contributed something and they got better. As theory expanded so did the accumulation of knowledge about the phenomena. Any theory is, by definition, a summary of existing knowledge, transitory, and a guide for research.

The book is intended to serve three purposes. First, it is an attempt to develop a model of deviance that synthesizes existing knowledge about it. Second, it is designed to imbue the model with empirical content so that through testing it can be verified and/or refined. Third, it can engage students in the process and thus the books attention to literature and the historical background of the concepts.

Several people were extremely helpful in the construction of the book though critique, editing and encouragement. Professor Thomas C. Esselstyn with his usual meticulous care was extremely helpful. Professor Michael Rustigan reviewed the work with a sharp and beneficial critical eye. Still the full responsibility for the content lies with the author.

List of Figures

List of Tables

CHAPTER I

INTRODUCTION

Theories of deviance are ubiquitous yet elusive. There have been many attempts at delineating such theories, though usually in micro-level or mid-level terms (e.g. white collar crime, mental illness or psychopathy). The major criticisms focus on the limiting nature of the conceptual schemes. They may fit one aspect of deviance but not all. Yet there are many overlapping concepts in the schemes and if coupled with the data from other socio-psychological sources, a synthesis may produce a more complete framework with empirical content for hypotheses testing.

Explanations for deviance have included the early traditional, bio-anthropological, psychological/psychiatric, and socio-cultural model. The essence of explanations in ancient times were the concepts of demonology and *lex talionis*; the more modern counterparts encompass the ideas of an omnipresence and expiation. The classical and neo-classical periods focused on rational man, free will and the principle of hedonism (Beccaria, 1819). The vulnerability of the hedonistic principle led to modification diluting free will as it blinded justice to extenuating circumstances.[1] The modern period began with the Positive School which argued that man's conduct was determined by his biological and cultural antecedents (Lombroso, 1918; Vold, 1958). The bio-anthropological explanations suggest that structure determines function. Deviant behavior is caused by some underlying

---

[1]For the modern counterpart of modified determinism see Tappan (1960: 268).

condition – glands, nervous system, or more vaguely, the constitution. These malfunctions are usually attributed to a defective heredity (Lavater, 1775; Fink, 1938; Hooton, 1939; Allport, 1937; Kretschmer, 1925; Sheldon, 1942, 1949). The most popular framework for explaining deviance remains the psychiatric/psychological one. Embedded in Freudian theory, this approach postulates that deviance is a consequence of personality, usually described as pathological (Freud, 1949, 1952). The myriad offshoots of Freudian orthodoxy have flooded the theoretical marketplace (Healy & Bronner, 1936; Aichorn, 1953; Abrahamsen, 1951; Yochelson & Samenow, 1976; Cleckley, 1964; Rogers, 1951; Glasser, 1965).[2] Opposing the psychogenic explanations of deviance is the socio-cultural emphasis on the environment. These schemes might include the effect on the individual of the structure of society (class, institutions), the social processes (competition, cooperation, consensus), the groups to which one belongs or aspires (family, peer, secondary), the culture and the subculture (values, norms, beliefs), and the reactions of an interdependent social system (audience reaction, social visibility of behavior), (Mills, 1943; Faris, 1955; Shaw & McKay, 1942; Durkheim, 1931; Sutherland, 1939; Merton, 1957; Cohen, 1955; Sykes & Matza, 1957; Cloward & Ohlin, 1960; Miller, 1958; Hirschi,1969; Lemert, 1967; Becker, 1963).[3] A model that synthesizes and circumscribes the promising aspects of this legacy and tenders empirical content for crucial tests should draw us closer to understanding deviance.

Although the variables used to explain deviance are too often treated as separate from the many forces in society, their interdependence are quite clear. For example, personality may be treated as separate from society but it still mediates between the self and society. The host of independent variables used to explain deviance tend to fall into three categories: personality, culture, and social structure, each broadly defined. The three categories in turn are related to each other to form a social system. A theory of deviance should not only suggest the specific variables, but also how they

---

[2]There are many others including the work of the experimental psychologists as B.F. Skinner.

[3]This relatively brief period of creative brilliance produced a huge inventory of literature of which these are some of the prime examples.

might be related so as to effect behavior or misbehavior. Another way of putting it is that deviance is a function of personality, culture, and structure; or $D = f (P \oplus C \oplus S)$, where D is deviance, P is personality, C is culture, and S is structure. Personality, culture, and structure are related to each other under all conditions. This relationship is largely a symmetrical one. It involves a processional sequence of continuous interaction. This is symbolically expressed as $\oplus$.

The model is in the form of $Y = f(X)$ where X is composed of X_{1a}, X_{1b}, X_{1c},....X_{1n}; X_{2a}, X_{2b}, X_{2c},....X_{2n}; and so on. This will help identify the paths, with stresses and strains, one negotiates along the conformity/deviance spectrum.

The model can be stated in the form of the following propositions:

Set 1.

1. The personality manifests a relative magnitude of conformity/deviance   potential.

2. The conforming/deviant personality potential experiences cultural   strain   toward   conformity/deviance   which intensifies or diminishes the conformity/deviance potential of the personality.

3. The   personality   potential   for   conformity/deviance, intensified or diminished by culture, is further effected by structural elements straining toward conformity/deviance.

Set 2.

1. The conforming personality exposed to a conforming culture in a conforming structure will conform.

2. The deviant personality exposed to a deviant culture in a deviant structure will be deviant.

3. The probability of deviance intensifies the more deviant the personality, culture, and structure.

The propositions derived from the functional model are a systematization of the process of becoming a deviant. It suggests that there are choices in behavior. These choices reinforce and are cumulative. Each accumulation changes the probability that a person will or will not become deviant. Choices are made by selecting from alternatives oriented by the characteristics of the internal (personality) and external (culture and structure) environments. The orientation is a product of socialization occurring throughout the life cycle, across the social system, by means of social interaction.

It could be argued that deviance is defined by its functions. But the model will delineate many paths on the route towards action – some of which will be sanctioned and others not. The literature indicates a variety of outcomes that are labelled deviant. Some are extreme, others narrowly defined. Cohen states, "The subject of this book is knavery, skullduggery, cheating, unfairness, crime, sneakiness, malingering, cutting corners, immorality, dishonesty, betrayal, graft, corruption, wickedness, and sin – in short deviance." (Cohen, 1966: 1). This broad definition emanates from norms as the source of deviance. However, deviance is more complex than that. Does it not also need visibility, social sanction, and other variables to explain it? Witness the increased use of deviance disavowal. Cutting corners can accomplish positive results, sins are religious attributions, unfairness is ambiguous, and so on. If there is any consensus on deviance, it includes mental illness, suicide, crime and delinquency. The functions of deviance are designed to establish a series of paths, with some more likely to lead to those patterns of behavior than others. Some outcomes may not be formally treated as deviant but have a strong potential for it. By formal is meant a sanction by some social institution other than the family. The model may suggest those actions that may become formally deviant and also those actors whose behavior is more likely to lead to formal deviance.

This general model does encompass a wide scope of human behavior. It is a conceptual scheme that abstracts significant aspects of social interaction. By no means does it encompass the whole human spectrum within the entire life space. For example, it may involve the consequences of socialization and institutional influence, but it does not account for their existence or their changes, or their differential impact.

The model involves abstractions expressed as concepts or perhaps more appropriately, as constructs. These short-hand symbols are characteristically vague, or as Blumer has noted, at best sensitizing. Their definitions are often moot, but traditionally expressed through an operationalizing process. The model permits a linkage, through operationalism, within an empirical framework. Thus, the conceptual scheme can be tested and adjusted and fed-back to model for improvement. Subsequent chapters identify specific elements of each construct and as variables are operationalized for testing.

Each dimension – personality, culture, social structure – circumscribe measurable variables for the discovery of each dimension's contribution to deviant potential. Assessing these measurements and coalescing them in the model will enhance explanation and conduce predictability with consequences for education and reform. The first signpost along the route is personality. As a product of socialization it reflects the influence of both culture and structure yet remains the vehicle with which one negotiates the social system.

CHAPTER II

PERSONALITY

With deviance as the dependent variable, two appropriate and interrelated features of personality are congeniality or congruence with conformity and personal coping mechanisms to handle stress. These properties of personality can be explored to assess personality's contribution to the model of deviance.

The literature abounds with definitions of personality. It usually refers to the dynamically organized system of personal traits; certain theorists might emphasize innate qualities, some learned ones, some both innate and learned ones, and finally there are those who would claim that there is no substantive and generalizable definition at all (Davis, 1949: 236; Yinger 1965: 141; Allport, 1937; Hall & Lindzey, 1957: 9). With this diversity one can feel comfortable singling out certain aspects appropriate for a given theoretical concern.

The framework for personality in this context is national character or the preferred term modal personality. A given culture contains certain uniformities which are transmitted through its institutions. These modal behavior patterns reflected in and by the personality (with individual differences) are used to distinguish one society (or part of a heterogeneous society) from another. This cultural milieu molds the person into a suitable personality for the particular society. Those that do not fit are more apt to deviate. It has been argued that the deviant has been incorrectly socialized or is within a subculture which is at odds with the larger society (Gough, 1947). In either case deviance may occur. The study of national character raises questions about the extent to which patterned life conditions in a given society (or part of it) generates distinctive personality patterns. The study of national character probably started with Benedict's "Patterns of Culture" (1934). This idea of the psychological coherence of the culture gave impetus to a large body of work (Bateson, 1942a; Benedict, 1946a, 1946b; Gorer, 1943, 1948; La Barre, 1946; Leighton, 1945; Mead, 1942, 1951). Psychology at first was hostile to this approach. However, by the mid 1950's they were able to accept the study of modal personality in cross-cultural perspective as an appropriate concern (Hall & Lindzey, 1957: 420-421). Sociology at first avoided psychological variables. Eventually they also attended to the relationships between personality and various aspects of society (Riesman, 1950; Inkeles, 1959, 1961; Smelser & Smelser, 1963; Ullman, 1965).

There have been several changes in and some disagreement with what is meant by national character. It has been variously described as "learned cultural behavior" (Linton, 1945, 1949), "basic personality structure" (Kardiner, 1939, 1945a, 1945b), "social character" (Fromm, 1941), and "configurational personality" (Benedict, 1946). The numerous definitions imply a common set of characteristics given society. There is some consensus for the term "modal personality" perhaps best described by Inkeles & Levinson (1969) as "relatively enduring personality characteristics and patterns that are modal among adult members of the society." There is also considerable consensus that societies are at least somewhat pluralistic so that national character is more apt to be multimodal than unimodal (Kluckhohn & Strodtbeck, 1961; Dai, 1948; Pettigrew, 1964; Devereux, 1951; DeVos, 1961). American society is indeed pluralistic with numerous substrata with personality, cultural, and structural differences. With the focus on conformity/deviance, certain modal characteristics will attract or detract from normative behavior. Since most people are conforming, the traits associated with them can become the reference against which congruence can be measured. For example, if flexibility is a conforming trait and a modal characteristic, those who score as rigid would be more apt to deviate. The measure can be more sensitive if the traits could be combined with the ability to use coping mechanisms. A series of traits would provide one score and the coping mechanisms another. They could be combined into an index to provide a sense of the personality's contribution to conformity/deviance. (See figure 2.1).

FIGURE 2.1

PERSONALITY AND DEVIANCE

Legend: P = Personality
P_t = Personality traits
P_m = Personality coping mechanisms
P_1 = Personality index
P_c = Conformity prone personality
P_a = Ambivalent personality
P_d = Deviant prone personality

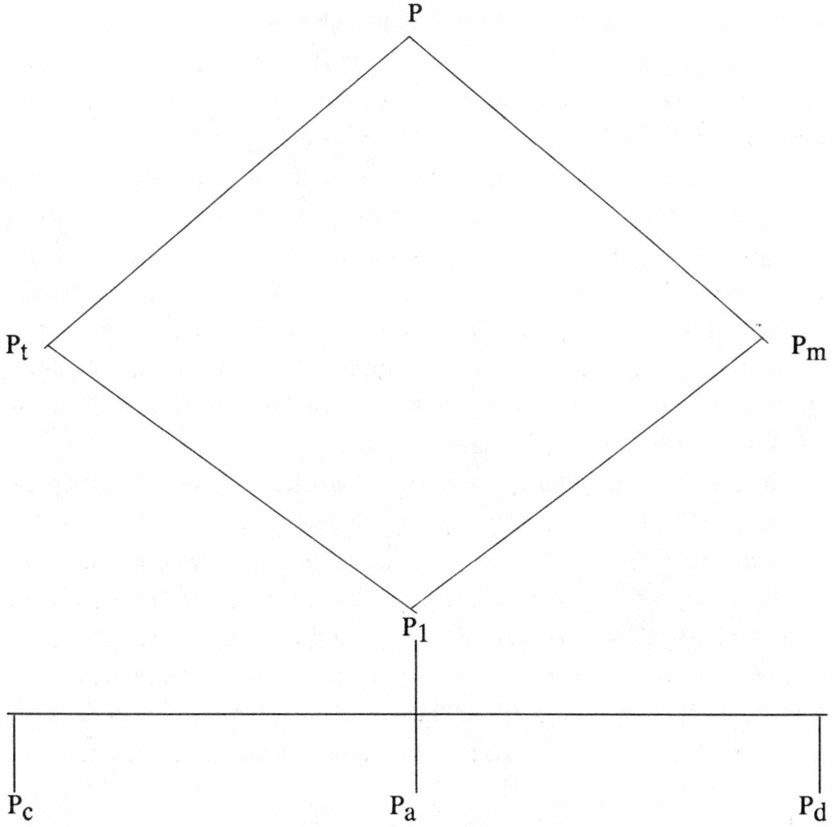

P

P_t P_m

P_1

P_c P_a P_d

RASMUSON LIBRARY
UNIVERSITY OF ALASKA-FAIRBANKS

Personality Traits

Any survey of the literature would attest to the prolificness of personality traits. The kinds delineated depend upon which dimensions serve as an arena. Some authors suggest types of personalities which seem to combine many dimensions and then contend one type as dominant in a particular culture. Riesman (1950) depicts the American character as other-directed, rather than inner or tradition-directed. The other-directed person has a primary concern with gaining the approval of others, possesses labile values in that they shift with the prevailing peer group standards, and responds to group sanctions with diffuse anxiety rather than shame or guilt.[1] Hofstede (1980) offers four dimensions of national culture: uncertainty avoidance, individualism, power distance, and masculinity-femininity. Morris (1942) in a somewhat different approach distinguishes three basic components of personality. First, there is the Dionysian component with the tendency to release and indulge existing desires. Second, there is the Promethean component with the tendency to manipulate and remake the world. Finally, there is the Buddhistic component with self-regulation and a check on desires. Each component is present in each individual in varying degrees. The Freudian influence directs attention to the developmental processes within the oral-anal-phallic structure. Child rearing practices are studied as the source of personality and modal characteristics. Studies within this framework claim importance of orality among the Marquesas (Kardiner, 1939) and the Alor (DuBois, 1944) and anality among the Japanese (Benedict, 1946a) and the Tanala (Kardiner, 1939). Also within the Freudian purview are ego and superego characteristics such as sociopathy (Gough, 1947) and self-rejection, self-esteem, self-derogation (Kaplan, 1975). There are many other traits directly or indirectly derivative of Freudian and neo-Freudian influences. Several complex traits are often explicated. Fromm (1963: 286) notes "tentativeness of autonomous choice" where the person faces dynamic polarities with the ability to leave choices open. Kardiner (1939; 1945b) suggests an "individual security system" with modes of adaptation (normative or nonnormative) through which one can gain group

---

[1]Sofer (1961) shows the relationship between Reisman's concepts and personality traits.

approval and support. The relationship to authority is an often noted correlate of conformity/deviance. Inkeles and Levinson (1969: 448) examine the authority-subordinate relations but with different kinds of authority such as legitimate and illegitimate. Inkeles and Levinson (1969: 472-473) illustrate a sham-guilt-ridicule axis. If a culture emphasizes guilt and a personality responds to shame, then sanctioning is less apt to be effective. Bergsma (1977) offers a sensitivity to social influences–a willingness to respond to pressures to conform. This represents the psychological counterpart to the effect of a social audience. Frustration and aggression seem obvious traits related to conformity/deviance. However, there is no evidence that the overwhelming number of deviants are overly aggressive. The key to these traits may be in the linkage with mechanisms of control.

Personality is a dynamic system and the associated traits are more apt to operate in patterns than in some simplistic single trait dominance or immutable hierarchy. There are some psychological arguments that the personality is an energy system and the chief function is activity to reduce tension (Sullivan, 1953). A major source of the tension is anxiety. The personality then is a homeostatic system with needs producing tension and activity restoring the balance. Can an abnormal anxiety level coupled with a diminished capacity to restore the balance be less congenial to conformity? Needs are not the only dimensions of personality. The literature includes cognition, perception, drives, motives, feelings, value orientations, and others.

There are many specific and measurable traits appropriate for an assessment of a conforming personality. Some of them are: industriousness, economic libertinism, discipline, orderliness, responsibility, self-esteem, self-derogation, dominance, dependence, empathy, autonomy, sociability, status-seeking, affiliativeness, power, sado-masochism, femininity-masculinity, capacity for change (flexibility, ability to cope, adaptability), efficacy (power to produce effects), individualism, egalitarianism, tolerance for ambiguity, gratification postponement, sensitivity to social influences, intellectual efficiency, and impulsivity (Montague, 1967; Kardiner, 1939, 1945b; Bateson, 1942b, 1944; Inkeles, 1966a; Lefley, 1972; Lipset, 1979). The focus should be on the trait and not the source. It should be hostility and not paternal authority. The traits should represent intra-personal characteristics with social relevance in that they are capable of impelling behavior. They should also have some reference in a modal personality and be measurable. The above list is not exhaustive but suggestive. Not all would be necessary to define either an individual or a modal personality. A subset that scans several personality dimensions would suffice to construct an index reflecting the degree of congruence with conformity. Such an instrument might include the following traits: self-esteem, sensitivity to social influence, capacity for change, impulsivity, hostility, responsibility, intellectual efficiency, socialization, anxiety level, dominance, self-discipline, and masculinity-femininity.

Coping Mechanisms

After establishing the contributions of the traits, a somewhat similar approach could evaluate two aspects of the individual's ability to cope: the quality and quantity of coping mechanisms.

Situational determinants like family cohesion impinge on personality. But so do other factors like coping mechanisms. A bad family situation may be balanced by good techniques to compensate. Coping is part of ego-development. It helps to mitigate shortcomings. Deviance itself is, at times, a mechanism for ego sustenance. These mechanisms may be psychological or cultural. The psyche may rationalize; culture may offer rule or role suspension. Both instances can relieve stress or strain. Some may be universal, but there is both personal and cultural diversity in terms of the alternatives available and which ones tend to dominate. Households may be physically divided for minimum stress, for some there may be some hope through a future, for others there is tradition perhaps backed by spirits.

Coping mechanisms are a system of behavior, a pattern which has certain techniques associated with it. The mechanism can be projection; the technique is to blame others. The mechanism and the technique may be normal or abnormal; it may be proscribed, prescribed, or tolerated. The concept of sanctions may involve barriers and punishment of various forms, but it also includes the availability and use of mechanisms to avoid sanctions or to handle them and in general to relieve stress, preferably in a prescribed manner. The greater the choice and availability of mechanisms, the more likely one is to placate the ego and relieve the stress. Kessler and Essex (1982) found less crime among married couples than single persons and attributed it to the greater number of coping mechanisms available and used.

The personality, as structured by the culture, uses a variety of mechanisms. They include: fantasy, rationalization, projection, denial, regression, reaction formation, verbosity (control situation and avoid stress), optimism, fatalism, avoidance, and many others. As was the case with personality traits, a subset of such mechanisms, within the context of specific situations, can be assessed. A paradigm of situations and the repertoire and quality of mechanisms used would permit the construction of an index reflecting coping expertise. (See table 2.1).

TABLE 2.1

SITUATIONS AND COPING MECHANISMS[1]

MECHANISMS[2]	SITUATIONS			
	HOME	OCCUPATION	PEERS	AUTHORITY
Fantasy				
Supression				
Rationalization				
Projection				
Withdrawal				
Denial				
Reaction formation				
Optimism				
Fatalism				

[1]A series of questions to assess each part of the table could be constructed.

[2]Each mechanism would be assessed for normativeness of use by measuring the degree or intensity of its application.

The coping measure combined with the personality measure provides an index of congeniality with conformity. The scores would permit three categories of persons: those with conformity prone personalities, those with ambivalent personalities, and those with deviant prone personalities.

From the myriad of measures of personality two interrelated components were selected to assess the function of personality for deviance/conformity. The two were: congeniality or congruence with conformity and personal coping mechanisms. Each aspect can be explored for empirical content. The traits suggested to assess congruence were: self-esteem, sensitivity to social influence, empathy, anxiety level, dominance, self-discipline, and masculinity-femininity. Most of these traits have been explored with valid and reliable instruments and normative references established. Coping mechanisms were examined in a similar fashion. A list of such mechanisms were suggested: fantasy, rationalization, projection, suppression, repression, withdrawal, identification, displacement, denial, regression, reaction formation, verbosity, optimism, fatalism, and avoidance. Again, existing instruments could assess some of these mechanisms, others could be constructed. Scoring each personality dimension in turn, standardizing the two results and then combining them into an Index of Personality would offer a score used to describe the conforming, ambivalent and deviant personality's contribution to the model.

CHAPTER III

CULTURE

Like personality, from the several aspects of culture a few can be selected and assessed as measures of a person's or group's affinity for conformity. Four such attributes are: beliefs, values, norms, and techniques of tension management – the social coping mechanisms that are analogous to the psychic mechanisms.

Perhaps the classic description of American conformity was offered by De Tocqueville in the 1830's. "It seems at first sight as if all the minds of the Americans were formed upon one model, so accurately do they follow the same route'" (De Tocqueville 1945: 273). His was a prescient source of the American personality arrived at through the culture. The ubiquitous influence of the majority rule as an implacable bulwark of democracy carved a path of conformity and standardization that helped bind the American character. Culture provides the arena in which personality is expressed. It provides the symbols for its expression and the techniques to meet stresses, strains, and conflicts which it helps to create.

However, apparent normative behavior in one culture (or subculture) may seem pathological from the perspective of another (DuBois 1944, Miner and De Vos 1960). Some disciplines attend more to inner functioning, others to social adaptation. Therefore, the same responses might seem pathological to one and normative to the other. Yet Sumner assumed a strain towards consistency as part of culture. Sometimes it is difficult to distinguish the norm from the pathological and what is universal from what is particularistic.

This difficulty exacerbates the empirical search for verification of theoretical statements. But the various perspectives are related and universalism as well as particularism does exist. There are ample studies of both pan-cultural and cultural specific symptoms of illness (DeVos & Hippler, 1969). Epidemiologically, cross-cultural patterns of suicide vary greatly (Murphy, 1959). Deviance needs to be understood within its cultural context. Yet cultural and psychological determinants of deviance are interrelated. Conflict between social demands and psychic needs is a dynamic relationship, in part mediated by social and psychological coping mechanisms. One attempt to integrate cultural and psychological determinants of suicide was the work of DeVos (1964). In reporting on suicide in Japan, he reformulated Durkheim's categories and included an extreme dedication to a social-occupational role (role narcissism) as a source of anomic suicide (Durkheim, 1951). The idea of juvenile delinquency probably emerged with industrialized societies (Mizushima & DeVos, 1962). This offers evidence of the interdependence of culture, personality, and even structure, all contributing to changes in rates and forms of deviance. Lin (1958) reported differences in patterns of delinquency between the middle and lower classes in Taiwan generated by contrary adolescent reactions to subcultures emerging from modernization or Western cultural contact. Such differences along class lines are also found in the United States. America may be effected by ethnic and racial frictions while Europe seems effected by mobility, urban congestion, social isolation, erosion of traditional standards, and a lack of a sense of security (United Nations, 1952).

All these factors suggest a mix of personality, culture, and structure. If theory can be applied to a specific social context (e.g. America) by establishing the modal personalities and dominant cultural traits and then indexing the congruence of specific individuals or groups, this can control for the various aspects of pluralism.

The definition of culture is as elusive as that of personality – and just as broadly conceived. The contemporary sense of culture was probably introduced by E.B. Tylor in 1871 (Tylor, 1958). Much later Linton offered an influential definition stressing integration,"...the configuration of learned behavior and results of behavior whose component elements are shared and transmitted by the members of a particular society" (Linton, 1945: 32). Controversy as to what it is still plagues the disciplines using it. In general, it is defined as the complete life style of a group–a social heritage. The various acquired products of a human society are included such as knowledge, beliefs, values, norms, skills, customs, and some theorists include artifacts as material culture. This heritage is both a product of action (effected by personality) and a mainspring of action (Kroeber & Kluckhohn, 1963: 357). Therein lies the relationship between culture and personality. The contribution of culture to deviance is illustrated in figure 3.1.

Beliefs

The several components of a belief system could by divided into three categories: philosophical/religious, economic/political, scientific/technological. Assessing a belief system would require the use of symbols within the three categories and the vigor with which people interact with these symbols.

Beliefs are cognitive elements – commonly held cognitions. Consensus includes them as an integral part of culture. They are ways of existential comprehending; the ethos of a society (Sumner 1960; Honigmann 1949; Bateson 1958). It signifies the nature of reality through language (Sapir 1961; Carroll 1956). The importance of language (especially meaning) is so paramount that beliefs are often referred to as symbolic culture. The system encompasses a world view, a *weltanschauung*, through a biased eye. This is not a view of the world in a geopolitical sense, but in an existential one. It is a sense of reality as the society defines it. On occasion a chronicler may define a society as he sees it such as Spengler's Faustian view of Western life or Redfield's view of peasant societies (Spengler 1926-1928; Redfield 1947,1957). The system of beliefs may be characterized as an ethos or themes or patterns that give direction to culture helping to establish prevailing norms and values (Benedict 1934; Hallowell 1960; Opler 1945; Merton 1957). Beliefs are effective patterns of culture shared in common but variously interpreted – creatively, idiosyncratically, or even destructively – with sometimes ambiguous conformity.[1]

---

[1]See Parsons and Shils 1951, especially chapter 3.

FIGURE 3.1

PERSONALITY ⊕ CULTURE AND DEVIANCE

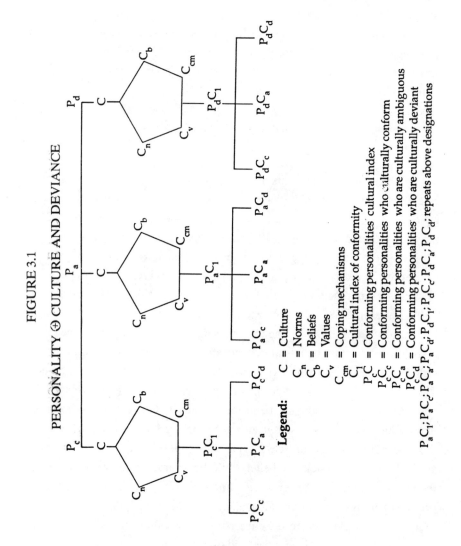

Legend:

C = Culture
C_n = Norms
C_b = Beliefs
C_v = Values
C_{cm} = Coping mechanisms
C_1 = Cultural index of conformity
P_cC = Conforming personalities' cultural index
P_cC_c = Conforming personalities who culturally conform
P_cC_a = Conforming personalities who are culturally ambiguous
P_cC_d = Conforming personalities who are culturally deviant

$P_aC_1; P_cC_c; P_cC_c; P_aC_a; P_aC_d; P_dC_1; P_dC_c; P_dC_a; P_dC_d;$ repeats above designations

Meanings are mostly a property of behavior. It is what we do with objects or concepts that give it the reality. This leads to different interpretations of reality. A chair is a chair only because we sit in it. Another culture may use it as a battering ram and it loses its meaning as a chair. Since we use symbols to refer to meanings, and the symbols and meanings are arbitrarily associated, symbols and meanings can be transitory (Berger & Luckmann, 1966; Blumer, 1969). And a change in the belief system reverberates throughout the culture. The essence of culture is symbols. "Man works upon his environment, both the physical and the social, to fashion a setting to which he can relate and which can be related to him, as a person. This, as we have suggested, is the culture-creating act. The product of this activity is a world of symbols." (Jaeger & Selznick, 1968: 660). The authors go on to suggest, "Culture consists of everything that is produced by, and is capable of sustaining, shared symbolic experiences" (Jaeger & Selznick, 1968: 663). Thus, central to culture is "expressive symbols," not just symbols. For some contemporary writers culture counts as its elements norms, beliefs, and expressive symbols. The emphasis has shifted from norms to expressive symbols as analogous to fundamental beliefs (Williams, 1976; Peterson, 1979). Jaeger & Selznick emphasize the evocative nature of expressive symbols. Some theorists use culture as nearly equivalent to ideology (Gouldner, 1976). It might be more accurate to equate beliefs with ideology.

Symbols are associated with the three suggested categories of a belief system: philosophical/religious, economic/political, and scientific/technological. The flag represents the political area, church for religion, microscope for science, computers for technology, and these are just examples of the many symbols attached to beliefs in a society. If the modal belief system can be described, then an individual's congruence with it can be calculated.

Of course each society possesses elements from each belief category. But each is differentially influential. Thus one society may be dominated by the philosophical/religious beliefs and another by the economic/political ones. Within the society one category may dominate for a while until another becomes more influential. At one time America was dominated by pholosophical/religious beliefs. In more recent times this dominance has been eroded by the influence of the scientific/technological category. At the same time, the political/economic beliefs have remained as a significant element in the culture. Russia has been dominated by political/economic beliefs but has begun to show the infection of scientific/technological beliefs.

A change in the belief system – a shift, for example, from the philosophical/religious to the scientific/technological, can induce strain on the values and norms so that they too will change. Most likely the value remains but with a lower priority or certain norms become less likely alternatives for action. Urbanization contributes to such an effect. Such characteristics as achievement and aggression may be reflected in both belief categories but there is a difference in the meaning and the way they are manifested. The focus of concern becomes more ego than social. Change can introduce stress as well as strain as influences clash and acculturation presents dilemmas.[2] One paroxysmal mechanism of social control to compensate for dramatic changes in beliefs is through some form of conversion. Thus conversion in a belief system – e.g. twice born – is a form of social control. Deviance itself may be a turbulent form of tension management. Perhaps this is clearest in the case of suicide.

The belief system may evolve concomitantly with other aspects of culture in a symmetrical relationship. But once formed it tends to dominate such other cultural elements as values, norms, and techniques for tension management. In the latter case, social mechanisms may become inadequate as beliefs change. No longer relieving tension, new ones are explored or old ones retrieved.

Once the reference for the society's cultural beliefs is established, including the distribution of the influence of each category, comparisons can be made with an individual or a group. Scores for each of the three categories would determine which one dominates. They could be combined into an Index of Beliefs, perhaps weighted for the differential impact. The scaling for each element of culture would be standardized so that they could be combined to measure concordance with the conformity-ambiguous-deviance classifications. Figure 3.2 illustrates the contribution of beliefs to the model.

---

[2]Strain would be in the system while stress would be in the individual.

FIGURE 3.2

ASSESSMENT OF CONCORDANCE WITH CULTURAL BELIEFS

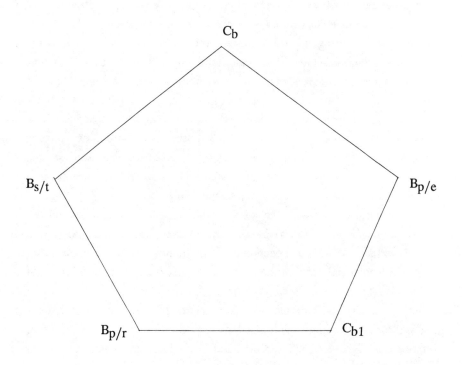

Legend: C_b = Cultural beliefs
C_{b1} = Cultural beliefs index
$B_{s/t}$ = Scientific/technological beliefs
$B_{p/r}$ = Philosophical/religious beliefs
$B_{p/e}$ = Political/economic beliefs

Values

In order to integrate values into the deviance model, it needs to be defined, empirically assessed, and incorporated into an Index of Culture. Exploring the concept should reveal its many facets from which appropriate variables can be selected.

Values always have been of some interest but few have pursued its meaning and impact with analytical diligence. The attribution of what is good often is directed to some supraempirical being–a thrust that could discourage an analytical approach. Thus values received some attention but little mastery. The definitions have changed, perhaps evolved, from early philosophical musing to sophisticated theoretical statements. In the contemporary view, values have been defined as widely shared conceptions of what is good; standards for desirable conduct; anything of some degree of worth to a specific group; principles that guide our actions. It sometimes has been used synonymously with interest. It has also been described as a phenomenon's objective meaning to group members with attitude as a subjective counterpart. Though we speak of shared concepts of what is good, the extent of the sharedness of each value may differ within a group, from one group to another, and across the society. But, the more the sharing, the greater the cohesiveness of the group. The more the value is shared the more people are apt to behave similarly. Shared values make possible a modal personality–or is a reflection of it. A commitment to common values contributes to social order–some argue it is a necessary condition for social order (Parsons, 1939). The importance of each value also differs and assumes a chimerical hierarchical arrangement. It effects behavior directly and indirectly; it induces stable patterns of interaction setting the standards for rules, a source of social predictability. There is still conflict. Values compete for dominance and the system has strains and inconsistencies. We value equality and practice discrimination. But values are not eternal qualities or intrinsic to an object or a principle, nor are they abstract entities. "In the light of concrete analysis it is meaningless to speak of values as if they existed independent of the valuating subject or the group for which they are valid," (Mannheim, 1957: 131). Values are existential, socially generated, and the rational products of insights into the needs of society.

Though contemporary work in value theory remains relatively rudimentary, it shows greater precision from its historical roots and subsequent evolvement (cf. Spates, 1983). Ibn Kaldun (late 14th century) was probably among the earliest of the social analysts to deal with some version of values (Boskoff, 1972: 173). He contrasted the nomadic community with sedentary ones. The former emphasized the values of solidarity, simplicity, and bravery; while the latter community emphasized luxury, security, and profit. However, the concept as managed in the socio-cultural arena was inherited from philosophy (as were so many other sociological concepts). For Adam Smith labor was the basic standard for evaluation. Marx developed a labor theory of value. The source of values was located in the class position. The first sociological definition is attributed to Thomas and Znaniecki (1921). They defined values as any datum with empirical content accessible to a group with the meaning applied through activity. Other sociological theorists bandied with the concept. Small and Vincent (1894) wrote of a "common will," Giddings (1907) of a "social mind," Sumner (1906: 38; and also Pareto) wrestled with values but quite obliquely. Sumner saw values as a consequence rather than an effect of norms. Pareto (1935) sought recurring themes or "residues" underlying rules and rites.[3]

In spite of this early interest, as a concept it lay more or less barren until Parsons (1951, 1939, 1953) gave it its modern focus and impetus and dominated the sociological thinking in this area until relatively recent competing alternative theoretical approaches. Social life was possible only with common values (Parson & Shils 1951: 165). Parsons (1954: 357) emphasized the role of value in action, not as the act of evaluation of an object, but as the standard by which the object is evaluated. These were his "modes of value orientations." Values were linked together in a system of orientations. Choices of value orientations were structured–i.e. the value choices were directed by pattern variables: universalism vs. particularism, ascription vs. achievement, self vs. collectivity, affectiveness vs. affective neutrality, and specificity vs. diffuseness.

Parsonian value theory strongly influenced and attracted other theorists (Kluckhohn, 1961); duBois, 1955; Williams, 1970; Kluckhohn & Strodtbeck, 1961). Clyde Kluckhohn (1951: 395) derived the contemporary definition: a conception, characteristic of a group, of that which is desirable,

---

[3]Anthropologists were also concerned with values. See Boas (1911), Radcliffe-Brown (1922), and Benedict (1934).

thus influencing action. Florence Kluckhohn (1950) offered further refinements. Values were hierarchal. Value orientations (different from Parson's notion) were based upon five common social questions: what is the nature of our relationship to other people; what is human nature; how do we relate to nature or supernature; what is the nature of time; what is the nature of activity? The answers produced a belief system that served as the basis for all other parts of culture (Kluckhohn & Strodtbeck, 1961). From this analysis American value orientations became: human nature was good and mutable; there was a commitment to mastery over nature; the time orientation was towards the future; doing had precedence over being; and gratification of the individual was primary in social relations.

Later, Parsons in another of his coruscating moments, added to the functional theory of values. Values were separated from norms. The former was an abstraction while the latter was specific rules for action (Parsons, 1961: 43). He also advocated a cultural impulsion towards the generalization of values. The values diffused throughout the culture and while sifting out value strains, became more acceptable and imbedded in the society and less and less mutable (Parsons, 1966; Lipset, 1963).

Needless to say this functional value theory met with ample criticism (Wrong, 1961; Blake & Davis, 1964). There was little empirical support. The abstract nature of the theory made testing and a search for empirical content difficult. Some studies were done but not enough to qualify as proof (Kluckhohn and Strodtbeck 1961; Smelser 1959; Kahl 1965; Spates 1976). In spite of the historical background, the many attempts at analysis, the attractiveness and ascending influence of the Parsonian approach, and the subsequent alternative theories, the role that values play in social life remains illusive.

Alternatives to functionalism produced other approaches to values. Myrdal (1944) argued a disparity between ideal and real values. Riesman (1950) demonstrated a value shift to an other-directed society. Some attempted a classification of American values (Coleman, 1944; Gillin, 1955). Research techniques emerged to analyze values (Vernon & Allport, 1931). Mukerjee (1966) suggested that values were multifarious and inconstant, at times in conflict and evolving from personal experiences as well as from culture. Becker (1950) argued that values formed from certain human needs – security, response, recognition, new experience – the sacred and the secular. Morris (1956; 1964) described thirteen main orientations. Catton (1959) combined the idea of values as a conception of the desirable and the idea of values exhibited by preferential behavior and developed a series of hypotheses for testing. By 1965 both functionalists and alternative approaches continued to struggle with the concept as disagreement and equivocation remained.

In more recent years, using sophisticated techniques, differential class values were explored (Kohn and Schooler 1969; Kohn 1977; Pearlin and Kohn 1966; Wright and Wright 1976; Glabb 1981; Slomezynski, Miller, and Kohn 1981). The higher classes were found to place greater value in self-direction for their children than the lower classes while the lower classes placed a higher value on conformity to externally imposed rules. Such studies are not new (Hyman 1953; Morris 1956). In spite of claims of significant differences, subcultural differences have not been resolved. Kohn and Schooler (1969: 676) in their analysis of social class differences noted, "much of the variation in men's values and orientations results from what we have to regard as idiosyncratic personal experience." Finding people who do not fit into some class mold is not unusual. Too many working class folk have middle class aspirations and use that class as a reference group. The value models are readily available through the mass media. There are also rallying points for, or at least lip-service to, ideal values which reinforce them. These include Christmas, Easter, Church, charity, social movements, voluntary organizations, and rites to be good. To practice a value depends on role, status, and opportunity. If it is not practiced, it does not mean it is not valued. One might focus on a different value as a substitute – at least it is a *substitute* –which may offer an ego defense, (see Kohn and Schooler 1969). Some roles require less compromise than others; the clergy cannot be drunk, the truck driver can. The former becomes a model for cultural values. Values are complex. Inkeles (1977) sees American values as stable while Bosserman (1977) sees them as fundamentally changed. They may be hierarchal, inconstant, relative to a situation, and legitimize and give meaning to norms. In the latter case, there are alternative norms that express the same value. The more developed the society, the more alternatives that are "valued" or at least are tolerated. All these convoluted choices can produce tensions – the more alternatives, the more difficult the choices. The simpler taboo system makes choices clear and deviance more easily defined.

The history of the emergence of value as a concept includes attempts at describing American values, and gathering them into categories. Williams (1970: 501-502) listed some American value themes: active mastery rather than passive acceptance, external rather than an internal world, an open rather than closed mind, rationalism not traditionalism, orderliness rather than disarray, universalism not particularism, horizontal relations over vertical ones (equality), individualism as opposed to group identity. Others have noted individualism, hard work, success, cleanliness, and a host of others.

Values can be categorized in terms of different types. Waller (1936) suggested two types: organized or basic types such as private property, monogamy, individualism, nationalism, christianity; the humanitarian types such as making the world a better place, or remedying the misfortune of others. The predominant value category seems to be moral, but others also include technical, aesthetic, rational, collective, and egoistic, the value patterns of Parsons, and universal kinds fulfilling basic physical needs (intrinsic).

Perhaps the most significant contemporary work has been done by Rokeach (1973; 1979). He designed a value survey to measure 18 "terminal values" (preferred "end states of existence" such as happiness and wisdom), and 18 "instrumental values" (preferred "modes of conduct" such as honesty and responsibility). His work has provided the most comprehensive study of American values and their association with such variables as class, age, race, religion, and subculture. He also explored value change and the relationship between values and behavior.

It would seem most efficient to adapt the Rokeach instrument to the assessment of the contribution of values to deviance. It would require a standard of values, controlled for race, age, and other similar variables. A comparison with this reference could produce a score that would reflect a deviant/conforming tendency. An Index of Values could be added to the other aspects of culture and contribute to the measure of culture's influence.

Norms

The basic values shape the goals of a culture or subculture for which certain normative patterns are seen as desirable for achievement. Do subcultures possess similar or different normative patterns which then are differently tolerated by the overarching culture? What stresses and strains then obtain, due on the one hand to a limited access to means and on the other hand to different ends? Then what mechanisms exist to ameliorate the stresses and strains? The linkage of values and action and reaction persuade the analysis of norms and their effect on deviance. The plethora of norms need to be identified, categorized, and then techniques derived to measure the consequences.

"Would you live with ease,

Do what you ought, and not what you please".

So Benjamin Franklin cautioned his readers of the 1734 Poor Richard's Almanac. Over 200 years later we can recognize his admonishment as directed toward a normative order.

Social interaction does not occur haphazardly but on the contrary, it occurs within a system of rules referred to as norms. It has been argued that without norms there would be no society; and that the study and understanding of norms was crucial for the understanding of social behavior and society itself. Durkheim and Parsons attributed social order to norms because the majority subscribed to the same notion of what conduct ought to be. This idea has been debated extensively and rejected outright by Marxist sociology (Wrong 1961; Klapp 1973).

The definitions of norms are plentiful, yet there is some consensus. It has been variously described as: rules specifying what is appropriate and inappropriate behavior; the ways in which a culture does things; the blueprints for behavior; shared standards of desirable and undesirable conduct; socially expected and accepted forms of conduct. The consensus defines it as shared conceptions of what conduct ought to be in a given situation (Gibbs 1981: 1-5; Birenbaum and Sagarin 1976: 11; Blake and Davis

1964: 456; Homans 1961: 46). A statistical definition that equates a norm with an average is rare. Instead, the consensual definition is evaluative. Though the definition may have a measure of consensus, the diverse properties attributed to norms indicate its complexity. Gibbs (1981: 17) suggests at least five major normative properties: personal evaluation, perceived evaluation, personal expectation, perceived expectation, and distinctive reactions to acts.

Most rules are not either or propositions but offer alternative routes to the same end. In rules about dress, depending upon prevailing styles, women may for a given event appropriately wear minis, midis, maxis, or pants suits without sanction. The more complex the society, the larger the number of substitutes for conformity to some rule. Though the range of alternative norms may be large, the tendency is to settle for a smaller number from which to make a selection. Associated with the norms are a system of sanctions which vary from mild disapproval to arrest and from the pat on the head for being good to a highly successful career. Normative behavior occurs within a given social context. A correct norm in one context may be less correct in another. Spit and polish is appropriate on the parade ground but not in battle. There are also normative paths for socially intolerated as well as tolerated unusual forms of behavior.

There is a rich assortment of norms both within and across cultures. Ordinarily they have some functional requirement. When they cluster around such a function they are often designated as institutions (Blake and Davis 1964). In addition to the rules of conduct, conformity and violation are also patterned (Williams 1970). Norms can relate to an end or a mean; they can be prescriptive or proscriptive. They are evaded yet subscribed to; they may depend on contingencies to be followed or denied. They can be explicit (law) or implicit (gentleman's agreement), vague or specific, rigid or flexible.

Although norms mean something that occurs regularly or what society has the right to expect, they have disparate degrees of acceptance. Some may be universal, especially ideal ones like monogamy, others apply to specific groups (eg. ethnic), while still others are more ephemeral. The sense of obligation also varies from norm to norm and from context to context although some attachments are less transient than others. Even if the norms are widely shared there are many different "ways of life." These "ways of life" overlap, but in congregation may seem to be more different than they are.

One reason for the diversity within a normative system is the attachment to status. People from other statuses may not have the opportunity to apply certain norms, but they still accept them as appropriate for those of a given status (and role). A priest is expected to practice sobriety (stress should be handled by prayer); the drunken truck driver elicits no surprise (stress can be handled by drinking). Of course the priest is a value carrier and his norms should be ideal; the truck driver lives in the "real" world and this is reflected in his normative choices. Another reason for the variety of norms is that the prescriptions and proscriptions can be fulfilled by different degrees of acceptable alternatives. As Gibbs (1965) has noted, generically norms have three attributes: collective evaluation of behavior in terms of what ought to be; collective expectation of what it will be; particular reactions.

Norms are not immutable. Some change gradually as old ones fade and new ones appear; at times old ones return to widespread use. Public norms are suspended with decreased activity and interaction (Nash 1981). Laws create new norms and new norms create laws; these are formal or institutional forms of change. Informal ways to change norms can emerge through spontaneous interaction, frequently from subcultures. They may not be deviant norms but still invoke resistance. The violation of norms is not necessarily deviant – it can be normative. To be deviant requires a strong reaction from a significant part of the public (Cohen 1966; Schur 1971).

Why do most people conform to rules? Even criminals live normative lives most of the time. There are a number of reasons for general conformity; conformity is incorporated during the socialization process; the opportunity to deviate can be infrequent; it is more convenient to conform; conformity is reflexive – the norm is taken-for-granted; there are rewards for conforming; there are penalties for deviating (Schutz 1964).

The multifarious nature of norms begs for categorization. And many such attempts have occurred. Sumner (1906) divided norms into mores, laws, and folkways. These do overlap and exclude many other types such as ritual, ceremony, and rites. But this represented a useful beginning. Conventionally three types of norms are recognized which are similar to those outlined by Sumner. These are mores, customs, and laws. Mores have moral or ethical connotations while customs usually do not. Laws are institutionalized rules. More gross divisions of norms specify them as cultural and social, or informal and formal, or noninstitutional and institutional. The informal or noninstitutional types arise spontaneously from interaction while the formal or institutional types are rationally designed by organized bodies.

Another typology distinguishes social and legal norms. The former (after Sumner) involves two major kinds, folkways with minimal feelings attached to them and mores with intense feelings attached to them. Legal norms also are divided into two major kinds, torts and crimes. The tort is a private or civil wrong while the crime is a public wrong. The crime is in turn divided into misdemeanors and felonies. The former is a less serious crime while the latter is considered a more serious one. These reflect public sentiment as does Sumner's version of mores and folkways.

The nature of norms and their various types maintain ambiguity and dissent among investigators. Nevertheless, it is difficult to escape the insinuation of norms in any theory of deviance; it is therefore necessary to establish some operational parameters for their inclusion.

Most classifications of norms do not capture their diversity and multidimensional character. They are likely to range from none (anomie) to extravagant (fanatical). In between would lie instrumental norms (technological), esthetic norms (secondary), mores (primary), and ethical, virtuous, noble norms (moral). Discounting anomie, there are five norm types: technical, secondary, primary, moral, and fanatical.

Relating the types to the levels of sentiment attached to them augments the composition of a normative system. Three levels of sentiment are postulated: pre-proscriptive, preferential, and permissive. The pre-proscriptive level refers to norms of minimum leeway – either exclusionary or acceptable much like a system of tabus. The preferential level of sentiments are the reaction(s) most likely to occur. Even though several acceptable norm alternatives may be available, the propensity is to choose certain ones to the exclusion of others. The permissive level is one in which the norm choice may be allowed but not necessarily approved.

The level of sentiment varies with the type of norm. There is some rigidity of sentiment attached to each norm type. For example, technological norms would be mostly permissive while the fanatical norm would be mostly pre-proscriptive. Table 3.1 illustrates this relationship.

TABLE 3.1

TYPE NORMS AND LEVELS OF SENTIMENT

TYPE OF NORMS	PRE-PROSCRIPTIVE	PREFERENTIAL	PERMISSIVE
Anomie	–	–	–
Technological	–	–	+
Secondary	–	+	+
Primary	+	+	+
Moral	+	+	–
Fanatical	+	–	–

– Absent

+ Present

The norms are not equally distributed among the types and the distribution would vary from culture to culture and time to time within the same culture. Primary and secondary norms would be the most prolific. The reaction to deviance and the volume of deviance also is likely to vary with the type of norm. In the reaction to deviance the relation between norm types and the social reaction to deviation from them would be linear ranging from a minimal reaction to technological norms and an inordinate reaction to fanatical ones. The volume of deviance would follow the same path as the distribution of norm types. That is, deviance would be greatest for the primary and secondary norms and least for the technological and fanatical ones. Figure 3.3 illustrates these relationships.

FIGURE 3.3

NORMS AND DEVIANCE

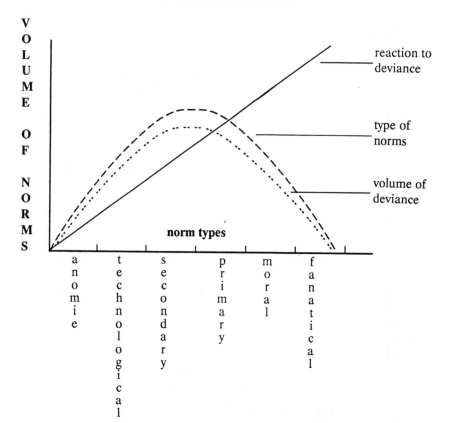

The normative system is an intricate one. As a variable in a theory of deviance an index or profile of the normative order of an individual or group needs to be developed. The various elements and assumptions can be synthesized to establish such a measure. A normative reference can be formulated either as a score or graphically as a profile covering several of the dimensions and then an individual can be compared to the reference. Then the categories of conforming-ambiguous-deviant will permit a placement reflecting the normative contribution to deviance.

From the numerous elements involved in determining a norm several major ones would establish a basis for assessing a normative system. But, at the outset, norms, unlike values, need to be defined in terms of acts. Where values reflect principles and are therefore abstract, norms reflect action – they involve doing. Lying on a beach in the sun may be a norm though it would seem to lack action. However, it is an act even though action in the physical sense is absent. A norm is doing something including doing nothing. The norm is the way in which we express ourselves.

One element of a norm is the arena in which we are behaving. This defines the situational dimension of norm use. Three such arenas are identified: interaction in the family, interaction with friends, and interaction in social institutions. Though these are not necessarily exclusive, they do offer extensive coverage of this dimension of a normative system. Another element radiates from what one does or will do in a given situation and what one thinks one ought to do. This element distinguishes real from ideal behavior.

A third element recognizes the significance of status and role. It covers the norm user to the norm producer; the value user to the value producer; the social status as reflected in the roles from family to institution in terms of leaders, followers, models, and influencers. The status/role dimension is summarized as Plebeian, Centurion, and Imperator – categories borrowed from the Ancient Romans. In this case the Plebeian status/role refers to the insubstantial intercourses and positions in which all occasionally participate. It might involve a social role in the arranging of a meal in a family, playing cards with friends, or digging a ditch at a construction sight.

As a role there is little evidence of a superior status but there can be evidence of an inferior one: the child in the home, the sycophant among friends, the blue collar worker in the occupational world. The Centurion is the median status/role – the wife in relation to a husband (in the traditional sense), the more skilled camper on a trip, the bureaucrat, engineer, or small entrepreneur. The Imperator is the preeminent status/role – the influential leader, a role aristocrat. Some examples would be the husband (or wife) in the patriarchal or matriarchal home, the social lion among friends, the politician in his seat, the doctor in his office, or the prelate in his church. We all fit in each category at different times, but one pattern or mode will dominate.

A series of statements can be constructed in each category of a paradigm relating all these dimensions. A dominant mode (or modes) would emerge as an index or as a profile and compared to a standard reference for assessment of the contribution of the normative system to conformity/ambiguity-deviance. Table 3.2 illustrates the normative profile.

The important cultural variable of norms can be measured for its influence on deviance. An intricate concept, it requires exploration of its many facets, and a synthesis of the levels of complexity. These levels include the situation for norm use, real and ideal behavior, and the status/role of the actor. The resultant gauge is then included in an Index of Culture and the contribution to deviance.

Cultural Coping Mechanisms

Everyone is faced with the challenges of social provocation. For some, the threat is most often successfully negotiated; for others, the task is fraught with failures. The difference is considerably dependent on a repertoire of coping mechanisms. The cultural capacity to offer a collection of ways to cope can be discovered and quantified for inclusion in the model of deviance.

TABLE 3.2

NORMATIVE PROFILE

STATUS ROLE	NORM TYPES[1]	FAMILY		FRIENDS		INSTITUTIONS	
		REAL	IDEAL	REAL	IDEAL	REAL	IDEAL
P L E B E I A N	technological						
	secondary						
	primary						
	moral						
	fanatic						
C E N T U R I O N	technological						
	secondary						
	primary						
	moral						
	fanatic						
I M P E R A T O R	technological						
	secondary						
	primary						
	moral						
	fanatic						

[1]Levels of sentiment are implied in norm types.

The personality encompasses mechanisms to cope with stress and maintain harmony and control. Culture (as well as social structure) also develops ways to enhance social relations to bate and prevent behavior requiring strong sanctions. Sometimes these techniques take seemingly bizarre forms – bizarre from an ethnocentric stance. Radcliffe-Brown (1952: 90-104) reports on joking ralationships – a relationship of "permitted disrespect" between relatives by marriage. This custom, most prevalent in Africa, is also present in Asia, Oceania, and North America. Combining friendliness and antagonism, the joking relationship could involve relatives by marriage such as a man and his wife's sisters, brothers, or both. The idea is to avoid conflict by maintaining a relationship based on levity. This controls interaction and keeps potential conflict at a social distance. Although complete avoidance is an alternative in some places, joking allows controlled contact. One relationship of some pertinence to our own society involves the husband and the mother-in-law. When restricted to "permitted disrespect" through joking, potential conflict is controlled. Radcliffe-Brown (1952: 136-152) attends to ritual avoidance of religious (taboo) and nonreligious kinds. Tabus involve sins; nonreligious ritual avoidance is concerned with good or bad luck. Tabus are obligatory; other ritual avoidance are optional.

Such coping mechanisms exist in American society both as a whole and within the various subcultures. Identifying and assessing these mechanisms and indexing a selection from them will complete the cultural contribution to the measurement of conformity/deviance.

Social interactions everywhere include a host of overt and covert ways to avoid a harsh outcome. The brilliant work of Erving Goffman (1967) designed to discover the intricate workings of social interaction – the nitty-gritty of presentations in encounters clearly exposes the subtle aspects of the pursuit of social harmony. He deals with mechanisms for maintenance of social organization and order. The rituals of interaction are designed to bind society together by binding the actor and recipient together. Some people and groups are better at this than others. rituals and ceremonies are examples of the mechanisms that contribute to order.

Goffman postulates two classes of rules: symmetrical and asymmetrical. The former includes a mutual sense of obligation and expectation. Asymmetrical rules lead to differential treatment between individuals. The difference is between substance and ceremony. Asymmetrical rules are for guiding conduct in matters of secondary importance. What is important is to express one's character or show appreciation of the other participants in an interaction. Not to steal from each other is symmetrical but the rule where a doctor gives a nurse an order and the nurse is not expected to give a doctor an order is asymmetrical or ceremonial. Two cases of ceremonial activities are deference and demeanor. Deference is "the appreciation an individual shows of another to that other..." (Goffman, 1967: 77). The rituals involve avoidance or presentation. Japanese bowing to each other sets a tone, and hopefully avoids anxiety and tension. Avoidance is ceremonial distance-keeping–it is what not to do. Presentation is what is to be done. The "How are you? Fine. Have a good day." exchange is presentational. Demeanor is ceremonial behavior conveyed through deportment, dress, and bearing. This reflects to others desirable or undesirable qualities.

Cultural attempts to control others, oneself, and the physical environment were elegantly traced by Sir James Fraser in the Golden Bough (1970). Within an evolutionary framework Fraser traced those conditions starting with magic, through religion to science. A prominent conception of social control was served by Sumner (1906) and with folkways, mores, and laws. Malinowski (1959) assayed primitive society and was convinced of the role of reciprocity for law and order. The binding obligation, the give-and-take principle in primitive society changes with the complexity of society; the more complex, the more manipulative reciprocity becomes. It also depends on the degree of personalization where the more intimacy (primitive society), the better it works; however, in modern society it still is impactful, especially in the primary group. We are vaguely aware that if we do not follow the rules, others might not and consequences could be discomforting. The Chinese distinguish two kinds of gifts, inexpensive and expensive. The former is a token implying no obligation with reciprocity relatively simple. The expensive gift implies obligation and reciprocity potentially begrudging and apt to roil the social encounter. Exchanging gifts in American society can on occasion jeopardize social harmony.

Reciprocity in modern society is captured in Goffman's (1967) face-to-face interaction ritual and the idea of techniques of neutralization (Sykes and Matza 1957). Techniques of neutralization can be cultural as well as psychological where social friction is circumvented and "face" saved through ceremonies, rituals, superstitions, magic, and reciprocity. Social control responses have moved from reflex to reflective, as suggested by Durkheim (1964) in the shift from mechanical solidarity to organic solidarity.

Spencer (1897: vols. 1, 2) also offered a theory of ceremonials. He denoted their differential aspects and showed that they generate from dominant-subordinate relationships. These ceremonies allay fear among subordinates and preserve inequality through symbolic control. Van Genep (1908) published his classic on rites of passage from one situation to another – usually along the life cycle. He distinguished rites of separation (death), rites of aggregation (marriage), rites of marginality (pregnancy, engagement, adoption). Ritual occasions enable the vacating of one role and assumption of a successor role thus alleviating stress and strain. Malinowski (1948: 29-35) pointed out the function of the funeral ritual as a means of preserving integration of the group. It counteracts death's disintegrating influence, a threat to cohesion, solidarity, tradition, and culture itself. The funeral ritual reintegrates the shaken solidarity and reestablishes morale.

Benedict (1938) contributed to the idea of discontinuity in cultural conditioning. She contrasted the roles of father-child where there are differences in responsibility-nonresponsibility and dominance-submission. In American culture the conditions for role changes are discontinuous, a kind of lack of training. One day one is nonresponsible; the next day one is expected to be responsible. What mechanisms are there for greater continuity, less stress and more conformity as a consequence? Does discontinuity contribute to fixation at some pre-adult level?

Ritual mechanisms that permit smoother transitions such as from adolescence to adulthood may reduce tensions with consequences for behavior. But caution is necessary in evaluating these rituals in the modern more complex societies. The rituals can be mechanistically practiced with meaning lost and effect inconsequential. The ritual passing may be no more than ostentation for parents and casuistry for the persons passing.

Lemert (1967: V) noted that older sociology tended to rest heavily upon the idea that deviance led to social control, "I have come to believe that the reverse idea i.e. social control leads to deviance is equally tenable and potentially richer premise for studying deviance in modern society." To extend this idea further, social control without the mechanisms for some degree of alleviation of the stress of control can stifle one into deviance. Social control with its rules is culturally designed as a sieve rather than as a wall. Garfinkle (1964) suggested that rules have an "et cetra" property. This is the process of determining the meaning of a rule when unanticipated contingencies arise within the context of the rule. Rule meaning involves an "intent" or "spirity" in addition to its instrumentality. LaPierre (1954: 124) noted "Every rule has, in effect, an 'escape clause.'" The child told not to play in the road but walks with one foot on the sidewalk and one in the gutter violates the "spirit" of the rule and yet has found the "escape clause."

According to Parsons (1951) in acute adjustment problems emanating from unusual strain, social control mechanisms (safety valves) block potentially disruptive reactions. Of course, access and opportunity are essential. Examples of such mechanisms flow from magic and religion. In bereavement, rituals can help abort feeling a loss of incentive and avoid disruptions (see also Malinowski 1948: 47-53). "Ritual...serves to organize the reaction system in a positive manner and to put a check on the disruptive tendencies," (Parsons 1951: 304). Ritual permits the symbolic acting out of tensions associated with stress within culturally prescribed forms. Parsons noted a series of "safety valve patterns" as elements of social control (1951: 270). Safety valves involve extra-permissiveness for certain behavior and emotional expressions not usually allowed, especially in adult or everyday life (e.g., grief at a funeral). Halloween permits mildly aggressive and even destructive behavior–trick or treat. Others include New Years Eve, Homecoming Games, Saturnalia, Rites of the Winter Solstice.

Parsons also cites youth culture as a "safety valve" which permits relaxation of stricter adult disciplines. When linked with major social institutions like education, some of the patterns of youth culture are legitimized through activities like athletics and dances. A great deal of youth culture is a process of emotional development–a search for independence, group loyalty, and gender identification.

Certain deviant roles are also tolerated–homeless people, certain kinds of alcoholism, and even mental illness. There is a "safety valve" in tolerance or legitimization of certain subcultural nonnormative behavior as might be evidenced through conditions like dress and life styles. Certain gambling functions serve the same purpose, especially "playing the numbers" or the latest craze, legitimate lotteries (McCall 1963).

The use of alienation and isolation as mechanisms of control present a dilemma. On the one hand, limited interaction decreases the need for control. For example, in prison isolation through avoidance is a way to stay out of trouble. On the other hand, it could be symptomatic of deviant potential and reduce the effect of social control mechanisms operating within an interaction arena. The answer is in the judicious use of alienation and/or isolation – that is, by the use of the mechanisms involved in these behaviors. Some examples are, the public behavior of the Japanese where one isolates oneself in a crowd; or the avoidance of eye contact in environments of potential strain (see Scott and Scott 1971: 103-135). Data suggests that culturally deprived persons avoid joining organizations, voting in elections, signing petitions, or keeping informed about current events. These could be signs of subculturally supported isolation and alienation. Avoidance mechanisms are significant in groups where persons are subjected to peer pressures and pluralistic ignorance. Certain groups accept ritual avoidance to ameliorate group loyalty and group pressure and reduce the potential for misbehavior (see Durkheim 1954: 230). In peer group and gang behavior role prescriptions offer order and social control. Is there a place or status for each person in the peer group or gang (Rosenberg in Scott and Scott 1971)? Some groups support the functional equivalents of deviance like nonmarital sex, risque entertainment, excitement, pornography, drunkenness, and certain drug practices. Sometimes dissimulation makes the tolerable intolerable by exaggerating uncommon behavior. Some ethnic subcultures (e.g., Asian American) react to a knocked over garbage can as if it were a major felony, particularly when their own children are the culprits.

Though groups, play, games, and pluralistic ignorance contribute to the development of social control, they are not the mechanisms but the arenas in which they are learned and used. Ross (1910), a pioneer in the area of social control, indicated some of the contributing arenas for social control as people negotiated the social gauntlet. Harmony, according to Ross, comes from sympathy, sociability, a sense of justice, and resentment. Social control comes from a number of sources – public opinion, personality, law, suggestion – all intertwined creating a dynamic social equalibrium with change followed by accommodation and then back to equalibrium. The sources are legion but related – taboos, ceremonies, rituals, myths, legends, dogma, fashion, advertising. Thus salient features can account for the impact of most.

The sources of cultural mechanisms for social control are legion and so are the mechanisms. Gossip controls. Its intent is to effect those who hear it by reminding the listener of approved behavior (Birenbaum and Sagarin 1976: 60). Rumor has a similar effect as does sarcasm (Birenbaum and Sagarin 1976: 61). In embarrassment a person tacitly says "oops, I goofed" and society sees this and says "O'K, we know and we won't react like it is deviance." Ostracism and exclusion like degradation ceremonies manage an event with high drama and humiliation and result in pressure to conform. There are various opportunities for catharsis – therapy, confession, gambling, sports, special friendly jousting, and many others. Subculture structures the form it takes. (see Rieff 1975: 392-410 for the role of psychotherapy in social control). There are recognized procedures for neutralizing stress like penitence, confession, repentance, and expiatory rites. Although it occurs in the sacred it can also occur in the profane. For example, Hispanics make use of a confidante in the gang. Conformity itself can be a mechanism of control, particularly as it pervades the youth culture. People tend to do as others do. Conformity is self-reinforcing; even if painful it can become a compulsion.

In addition to isolation and degradation there are expressions of reprobation or derision. There are many ritual practices, often mere superstitions (reaction to spilt salt), that reduce tensions. These ritual practices are especially useful in situations where the subject feels that there is no control ever events. Many of these rituals are pancultural. In a technological society, the religious or pseudoreligious rituals can be important as secondary rather than primary functions. A marriage ceremony does less for binding a marriage than for the family, economics, status, and social values. Rites are complex in consequences and function. The old idea of sanctuary still exists in modern dress as privileged places for tension management. These places offer the opportunity for role dissipation. Such places as chapels (in prison), recreation room (in mental hospitals), and in contemporary times various exercise establishments, all serve the same purpose. Many ceremonies like gatherings based on tradition–dinners, parties, family get-togethers are cultural devices to maintain morale, harmony, cohesiveness. However, mechanisms like these, and others, can encourage deviance as well as conformity. For those in a deviant group, rituals can support the deviance–the Mafia is a good example of this premise. Assessing cultural mechanisms of social control must account for the kind of group to which one is bonding. This is incorporated in the Sutherland idea of differential association.

Cultural mechanisms of social control have been recognized in one way or another by many observers of society. One can distinguish between sources, arenas, and mechanisms, and differentiate between cultural and associational mechanisms. The source is the impulsion for cultural coping; the arena is the context in which the coping occurs; the mechanism is the act which constitutes the coping. Religion is the source, the arena is the church, and the mechanism is confession. The avoidance of eye contact is the mechanism, social interaction the arena while the source could be psychological or subcultural pressure for anonymity. Assessing cultural copings could include the source and mechanisms with the arenas usually implied or specified for clarification. The sources, arenas, and mechanisms are diverse, often complex and covert, interrelated, and strikingly abundant. Many have been noted above: rights of passage, deviance disavowal, transitory redefinition of rules and roles, transitory suspension of rules and roles (including cultural fictions like disowning a family member), transitory fexibility of rule and role hierarchy, sanctioning networks (extended family), cultural stress of anonymity-intimacy or isolation-gregariousness, stigma management, dispute arbitrators (elders), ritual recreation (gambling, television, bowling, jogging, lifting of weights), circumspection in social interaction, special days and places, humor, buffoonery, gossip, rumor, sarcasm, reprobation, derision, deference, demeanor, reciprocity as structured by culture, sundry cathartic opportunities (confidante, priest, psychiatrist), functional equivalents of deviance (sexual freedom, pornography, certain drug use), dissimulation, rituals for solidarity (family albums and gatherings), mercurial tolerance of social roles (fanatics), and a multitude of others.

In order to express the impact of cultural coping mechanisms on deviance/conformity the spectrum can be categorized and a sample abstracted for heuristic purposes. Such categorization would be difficult to construct as so many of the mechanisms are recondite and encroach on each other. However, four categories: cathartic, collective, egoistic, and transitory, assessed across self, family, peer, and social institutions would reveal a faire mosaic of the texture of cultural copings. (See table 3.3).

The construction of the device to assess cultural coping should meet three conditions. First, subcultural variations can be evaluated in the categories involving family and peers. Second, the responses should reflect the kind of groups to which one is bonding. For example, one must distinguish between pursuing coping mechanisms to perpetuate a criminal career and to avoid deviant acts. Third, the responses should identify the degree of amelioration of the strain toward deviance.

Egoistic coping might include deviance disavowal, buffoonery, humor, functional equivalents of deviance in the self category; deference, demeanor, gossip, rumor, in the peer category; dissimulation, continuity-discontinuity in the family category; stigma management and circumspection in the social institution category. Collective coping could include in the self category, anonymity-intimacy, and isolation-gregariousness; reciprocity, derision, and reproval in the peer category; rites of passage, sanctioning networks, rituals of solidarity in the family category; dispute arbitrators and deviant social role tolerance in the category of social institutions. Cathartic coping might include in the categories of self, peers, family, and social institutions, ritual recreation, confidantes, tension management, and counselors, respectively. The transitory coping could include role redefinition in the category of self; role and rule hierarchy in the peer category; role suspension in the category of family; rule redefinition, rule suspension, and special days in the social institution category.

TABLE 3.3

SOME CULTURAL COPING ALONG THE SOCIAL GAUNTLET

COPINGS	SELF	PEERS	FAMILY	INSTITUTIONS
Egoisitic	deviance disavowal humor buffoonery	deference demeanor gossip rumor	dissimulation continuity-discontinuity	circumspection
Collective	anonymity-intimacy isolation-gregariousness	reciprocity derision reprovement	rites of passage sanctioning networks	degradation-amelioration ceremonies
Cathartic	ritual recreation	confidante	solidarity rituals	priest psychiatrist
Transitory	role redefinition	role hierarchy rule hierarchy	role suspension	special days

There are scores of cultural mechanisms to cope with the stresses and strains associated with everyday life. Those who have the opportunity and capacity to use them are more apt to be conforming than those who do not. The difference between the success and failure can be measured by categorizing the mechanisms and analyzing their use in various social interaction situations. Responses to an appropriate device – questionnaire, Q-sort – could approximate the degree to which one can guard oneself in the strain toward conformity/deviance. The resultant score can be related to the other aspects of culture's contribution to the conformity/deviance equation. The outcome can be used to complete the Cultural Index – beliefs, norms, values, and coping – and assess its offering to conformity/deviance.

CHAPTER IV

STRUCTURE

Structure is the final major dimension in the deviance mode. Again, the plan is to fathom the concept structure and then operationalize specific aspects for measuring, indexing, and combining the results with personality and culture.

The definitions of personality, culture and social structure share the same weakness – ambiguity and confusion. But, there is still some consensus in meaning and use – at least as a "sensitizing concept" for heuristic purposes. The term social structure is used in several different ways, many of them very vague, some narrowly focused, others more broadly applied.

The concept has gained wide currency when broadly used but discussions are invariably polemical. The term has appeared in the works of Spencer (*Principles of Sociology* 1885) and Durkheim (*Division of Labor in Society* 1893), in Mannheim's *Ideology and Utopia* (1936), and R.M. Mac Iver and C. H. Page's *Society* (1950). Some writers attempted to develop and refine the concept such as Radcliffe-Brown (*On Social Structure* 1940) and S. T. Nadel *The Theory of Social Structure* 1957). The idea was not accepted by everyone as Linton and Lowie omitted the term in the *Study of Man* (1936) and *Social Organization* (1948), respectively. Kroeber questioned its usefulness.

If there is a common thread in the several definitions of structure it refers to a pattern or network of relationships in a social system. Radcliffe-Brown (1952) includes all social relations in person to person interactions.

This includes kinships with dyadic relations and its consequent network. Social role and its consequent differentiation of individuals and classes is also an aspect of social structure, demonstrated by such as a division of labor, male-female and employer-employee differences. Smelser (1967: 6), from a structural-functional perspective, defines structure as "identifiable patterns of roles that are organized primarily around the fulfillment of some social function or activity." Thus, the educational structure involves roles organized to transmit culture; the economic structure involves roles organized around the production and distribution of goods and services. Parsons (1957: 67) in less lucid but similar manner defines structure as "any set of relations among parts of a living system which on empirical grounds can be assumed or shown to be stable over a time period and under a set of conditions relevant to a particular cognitive enterprise." (see also Kroeber and Parsons 1958: 583). Various other definitions include: a total network of understandings within a society; a general framework for networking and patterning; structure as interaction and its regularities; and opportunity and institutionalized means as another aspect of structure.

Social life is constantly renewing social structure. Relations are changing–there are births and deaths, marriages and divorces–yet continuity and stability endures. The idea of social relations assumes that the interaction is more or less reciprocal with structural adjustments occurring. Social institutions are the complex parts with which structure itself is reducible to social relationships.

In short, social structure is the way a society organizes itself or the way sets of relationships organize the society into, more or less, a viable entity. From this idea, three salient features of social structure that can be operationalized to assess deviance are role, status, and associations. This will be explicated in the following sections.

Role

"All the world's a stage, And all the men and women merely players; They have their exits and their entrances; And one man in his time plays many parts, His acts being seven ages." (Shakespeare, *As You Like It*, Act II, Scene 7). The analogy between theater and social life has often been suggested – Montaigne and Shakespeare through the modern writers Mead, Thomas, Znaniecki and Goffman. Moreno introduced psychodrama as a therapeutic technique from his dual background in theater and psychology. The term role is itself borrowed from the theater as are other terms such as person (persona was an actor's mask). The term role is more precisely understood and used in the theater than in social science.

The literature on role is voluminous yet obtuse. In spite of growing consensus, the concept remains enigmatic. Perspectives on role are so numerous and varied as to defy classification. A different perspective and/or unit af analysis leads to a different set of variables.[1] Although a difficult concept to use vigorously, it remains essential for descriptive and heuristic purposes and a crucial basic concept in sociology. The concept role probably derived from an approach in which interaction depended on what people believed themselves and others to be (Znaniecki, 1965: 20). From ideas derived from the works of Baldwin, Cooley, and Mead, the representation of self became a product of social interaction and communication. Mead (1934) claimed the basis for the perception of self came from the perception others had of us. Park and Burgess in their *Introduction to Sociology* defined the person as one's conception of one's role and concordant behavior. The early sociologists regarded role as a unit of socialization and personality or self as the internalization of roles. Their general idea of roles as a pattern of attitudes and actions in social situations left an oracular legacy. Attitudes are inferences about covert behavior or thoughts about behavior while actions are observable, thus divining a heterogeneous concept. Mead (1934) laid the foundation for theories of the self and role. He gave us the idea of "taking the role of the other" and the development of a role-taking ability. This ability is based on the responses of others toward the individual, communicating a view of self other than one's own. Mead's contribution to the idea of role was considerable. He used "role" to describe the process of cooperative behavior and communication.

Another significant influence on the general concept of social structure, as well as specific one of role, came from the work of Linton

---

[1]See Biddle and Thomas (1966): 21-63 for a summary of variables.

(1945). He directed attention to status and role as basic social structure; he defined role thus,"...includes the attitudes, values, and behavior ascribed by the society to any and all persons occupying the status," (Linton, 1945: 77). Newcomb (1950: 281) following Linton suggested, "Roles thus represent ways of carrying out the functions for which positions exist–ways which are generally agreed upon within the group."

Znaniecki (1949) defined groups as a synthesis of its member's roles. He defined social role by comparing it to a theatrical one (as did Goffman). Every social role like a theatrical one has a social circle within which the individual performs. Social roles are culturally patterned (i.e. they follow norms and values). Within these patterns, there are variations. According to Znaniecki, the four components of social roles are: person, social circle, duties, and rights (Znaniecki, 1965).

Goffman (1959) brilliantly presents a dramaturgical view of social interaction with the principles in theatrical performances playing roles on a stage. Parsons' (1951) pattern variables are explicitly designed to describe role-orientations. Finally, as the concept grew, Merton (1957: 368) noted that the structure of role and status provided the context for reference group behavior.

As role became increasingly useful, it also became increasingly complex. Common to most definitions of role are: social location, behavior, and expectations. Turner (1968) offers some general propositions on role:

1. Every role tends to acquire an evaluation.
2. Once stabilized, role structure tends to persist.
3. In organizational settings, roles tend to be linked to statuses.
4. Individuals tend to be assigned and assume roles consistent with each other.
5. Individuals tend to form a self-conception by identifying with certain roles from their repertoire.

Levinson (1961: 302) indicated three specific senses in which role was used. First, as structurally given demands associated with a specific social position (norms, taboos, obligations and other factors characteristic of the environment). Second, as one's orientation or conception of the part one is to play in an organization. This view is one that is characteristic of the actor.

Third, also characteristic of the actor, are the actions of individuals in terms of their relevance for the social structure. Levinson indicated that most writers embrace all three meanings and then shift from one meaning to another. He argues for treating each meaning separately.

Nisbet (1970) discusses the several attributes of role. It is patterned ways of behaving; it embodies norms; it is part of a system of interactive relationships; it has legitimacy (behavior is accepted if it proceeds from a role considered legitimate). It has an element of duty and authority. All of the above attributes are vital to any social role.

Some writers do not distinguish role and status while others see it as two sides of the same coin—a behavioral expectation to a particular relationship or expected behavior by particular people. Linking role and status seems to be the consensus definition—a pattern of behavior associated with a social position specifying the rights and duties of that social position.

Rules and roles also have been closely linked by theorists. Roles are prescribed and proscribed by norms including legal ones. Teachers do not perform brain surgery. Role is the total norms linked to a particular task or position.

It is also alleged that roles help organize behavior whether assigned or acquired. Roles are efficient ways to behave. They save time and energy, control ego strains, harmonize and synchronize interaction.

Role is often compared with personality. Personality is conceived as the sum total of the role repertoire. Broadly visualized, role theory holds that behavior is best understood as a function of role and personality. Personality and role relate to each other in a complex manner. One may be passive but need to play an aggressive role. A President or King, a general or soldier needs to perform aggressively but may have a passive core. In the reverse, the aggressive employee, servant or housewife may need to be passive and meek. Role and personality can thus be in conflict.

"Identities are socially bestowed" (Berger, 1963: 100). This captures the significant relationship between a social role and one's self. The role is sustained in a social context where what one thinks one is, is corroborated by the recognition and acceptance of the role, by others. The deviant, in this context, would very likely possess a damaged self-image. One of the earliest statements about the nature of self came from Charles H. Cooley in his major work *Human Nature and the Social Order* (1922). George H. Mead explored self further including the process of its emergence. Roles structure behavior. The self emerges from exposure to the many roles in one's culture. This occurs in the process of social interaction. In cases of role impairment, what is the reaction of the self? The self can withdraw, react by pursuing and projecting, or accept the definition of self. Lemert (1979) demonstrated how prolonged enactment of a role contrary to the expectations of others changed the identity and self of the systematic check forger.

Social roles are learned in the socialization process. Not just in the family, but in other social institutions as well. Roles are learned on the job, in the military, in church, and many other circumstances. Roles emerge through formal or informal social interaction. Symbolic interactionists (a term coined by Herbert Blumer in 1937) emphasize role construction through an interaction process. Labelling theory, borne out of symbolic interactionism, emphasizes role construction by attending to the shaping of behavior by expectations of those with whom we interact and the reactions to the assignment of labels. According to Erikson (1957) role acquisition involves two processes: role validation and role commitment. Role validation is the community expectations of a person's conduct within a certain status. Role commitment is complimentary to role validation where a person adopts a behavior style committing self to role themes reflecting a social position. Role preparation may show continuity or discontinuity. For example, a delinquent's role preparation might be followed by continuity and adult criminality or discontinuity and law-abiding citizenry.

Role models, who they are and their impact, is a measure of potential role performance. Role models, opportunity and exposure as a link to deviance, was assessed in families by Jessor, et al (1968: 259-260). However, such studies need a broader base to include other social institutions. Similar to the role model is the idea of representative role. This role involves a person in authority in an organization who represents the organization to those below him. It could be a role played within a collectivity or to other persons or other collectivities (see Kemper, 1966; Parsons, 1951: 100;

Parsons and Olds, 1955: 204). Such roles can lead to the idealization of expectations relating to the organization.

Roles are generally institutionalized. In a changing society there are always emerging roles which in turn become institutionalized. Submerging roles fade away, at times to emerge again, at other times, to disappear. Roles also change internally, people age, change careers, divorce, marry, have children, and so on. Rudoff and Devos (1970) illustrated family role differences and changes cross-culturally within the same society.

The number of available roles in contemporary society are legion, and the choices almost infinite, though controlled by such variables as status and opportunity. Several attempts have been made to order the number of roles into types. Nisbet (1970: 165-180) denoted what he considers the major social roles in history. The Patriarch is characterized as possessing age, wisdom. power, nurturance, and affiliativeness. The Prophet is characterized as possessing authority on the unknown, as interpreter of the sacred with moral superiority. The Magician is characterized as possessing arcane power, special knowledge and ability to effect the natural order. The Warrior-Chief possesses strength, youth, cunning, and courage. The Political man is responsible to a social entity. The Man of Knowledge has mastered the self, and pursues knowledge for its own sake. The Artist searches for beauty, communicates and interprets. The Entrepreneur has energy, foresight, and skill. He breaks out of the social order and directs an enterprise. The Rebel is intrepid, bold, and possesses considerable acumen. Of course most people, regardless of the historical period, do not play these roles. Some may have elements of the characteristics and receive high evaluations by others. Roles of this nature have changed as have their evaluations.

The literature often discloses examples of social typing. It shows examples of role-playing types such as inmates, criminals and other deviants. In addition to deviant role types, there are disvalued role types – those of low status, undesirables, and similarly negatively defined roles (see Scheff 1966; Edgerton 1967). From a labelling perspective, deviants are singled out through role differentiation and allocation (Turner 1972: 308). Szasz (1961) asserts that most mental disorders are social roles. Turner (1972) indicated instances of deviant role avowal where it is the lesser of two evils. Goffman (1961) refers to the disidentification of a person with the activity he is engaged in such as an adult fatuously doing something childish to create distance between the act and the role.

Nadel (1957) also identified several role types. Recruitment roles involve behavior based on such characteristics as age, sex, origin, and descent. Kinship roles involve relationships among relatives. Achievement roles have several sub-types: proprietory includes possession of skills, resources, and learning; expressive involves beliefs, creativity, and communication skills; service encompasses occupations; relational identifies partners, rivals, authority, leadership, and patronage.

Shibutani (1961: 326) distinguishes between conventional roles and interpersonal ones. The former is the standardized and impersonal roles with rights and duties habitually similar regardless of who plays the role (e.g. teacher and student in the classroom). The interpersonal role is one in which the claims and obligations depend entirely on the personal characteristics of the participants (e.g. teacher and student in a dating situation).

Cohen (1966: 13-15) differentiates two major types of roles: collectivity roles such as Catholic and male; roles within a collectivity such as teacher and parent. Maxwell and Hage (1970) developed a typology of role relationships. The analysis generated three major dimensions for describing role relationships: intimacy, visibility, and regulation. From these dimensions emerged an eight fold typology of role relationships which were, in turn, related to Tönnies Gemeinschäft and Gesellschäft distinction. Intimacy was defined as "concord" of "family spirit," the opposite of "public life." Visibility and regulation are variations on the gemeinschäft-gesellschäft theme. From a social control perspective, intimacy requires less visibility and regulation. Toward the other end of a community-society continuum, visibility and regulation loom larger for social control.

The concept of role itself has been expanded by fragmenting its characteristics. The number of roles in one's repertoire has been linked to the ability to adjust. A plurality of roles is universal, but the more complex and differentiated the society the greater the number of roles. The greater the number of roles, the more opportunity for strain and conflict. However, to counteract this, there is bound to be a development of role stress management, a complex skill differentially distributed in population and in opportunity. One study indicated a relationship between pathological behavior and a paucity of roles (Cameron 1960). Another study found that authoritarianism is negatively related to the number of social roles mastered (Stewart and Hoult 1970). The difficulty in dealing with role numbers is in determining when it is too large and when too small.

There are other aspects of role, some to clarify meaning, others to explore variables. Roles are usually described as complimentary – superior-subordinate, teacher-student, father-son. The reciprocal nature of roles is said to contribute to social control because it encompasses duties, responsibilities, and obligations. Proper role play has its rewards; improper play its sanctions.

Merton (1957: 369-370; 1967: 41-42) defines role-set as "complement of role relationships which persons have by virtue of occupying a particular social status." The single status of teacher includes roles of colleague, employee, and others. Each status has its role-set. This is differentiated from multiple roles which refers to a complex of roles associated with many statuses. A socially patterened status is a status sequence. For example, there are statuses successively occupied by student, graduate student, assistant professor, associate professor, professor, dean, and perhaps college president. In summary, role-set is where each status involves an array of roles; multiple roles are those associated with various statuses.

Merton (1967: 371-379) refers to certain mechanisms for articulation of roles in a role-set to produce higher degree of social order. Order is diminished and stress increased if, for example, one person in a set possesses a power monopoly. Some of the mechanisms to reduce stress are:

1. Differing degrees of involvement in role relationships among those in role-set balances the intensity of involvements.
2. Differing power allocations in a role-set avoids a power monopoly.
3. Insulating role-activities from observability by certain role-set members permits role behavior at odds with some members.

4. Social support by similar others in a social status with similar coping difficulties.

Everyone has access to interaction but crucial for behavior or misbehavior is carrying off the parts to be played. Thus the interaction arena becomes a source of stress or harmony. The degrees to which one is able to adequately fulfill the roles becomes a measure of role performance. Is the role performance impaired or successful if not eminent? Adequate role performance requires sustained identity, poise, and mutual confidence (Gross and Stone 1965). Each role performance has many variations but the variations are not infinite. They could become deviant or socially unacceptable.

The adequacy of role performance is linked to one's role-taking ability, another measure of the impact of role on behavior and misbehavior. There are extensive differences in the ability to take the role of the other. Role-taking consists of recognizing others as objects capable of independent action, appreciating the others' subjective experience and appreciating the range of responses in a given situation, then projecting one's own experience on others. If there is one concept that captures the essence of role-playing it is in the technique of empathy, although empathy and role-taking are not synonymous. There is a difference between the role itself and how one plays it. How does the behavior fulfill the expectation? Not that the expectation is rigidly and singularly defined, but within a range of expectations. Proper role-playing is evaluative and dependent on alter-ego or alter-group, indicating the plurality of each role. And each role-taking experience is related to many variables among which status is crucial.

The potential for mishap in the role-playing, role performance experience is extensive, although not always crucial for deviance. Goode (1960) developed a theory of role strain defined as the difficulty in fulfilling role obligations. He argued that since the total role obligations are over-demanding, strain is normal. However, many mechanisms are available to reduce the strain. Goode suggested several sources for role strain and some mechanisms to alleviate the strain. The sources are: no role demand leads to automatic conformity; all people engage in many different obligations; each role relationship requires several activities or responses which may be contradictory; many role relationships are role sets leading to a wide array of role obligations. Some of the mechanisms to alleviate role strain are: ignore the problem of role consistency; delegate some of the role obligations; eliminate a troublesome role relationship; setup barriers to continuing or initiating role relationships.

Gross and Stone (1965) found embarrassment incapacitates role performance. Deliberate embarrassment (e.g. children or adults often "trick" others) serves as a way to socialize skill in maintaining and reestablishing poise. There are other sources of role strain. An important one is in the depth of the shared conception of the roles between alter and ego. For example, how well does the conception of the husband and wife roles harmonize or empathize? Role conflict can be an outcome of poorly shared role conceptions or a source of strain itself. The conflict can occur within the self as well as between two or more people where role expectations are not met.

Gibbs and Martin (1958) offered a theory that postulated that role conflicts vary directly with the extent of incompatible statuses; and incompatible statuses vary inversely with the degree of status integration. This suggests the importance of role conflict for deviance. Status compatibility refers to the amount of role conflict in a person's various statuses. This is different from status inconsistence where inconsistency can relieve the strain of low status. For example, the person earning a living shining shoes can be a "King" in his own home, or an important Moose at the local lodge. This status inconsistency can ameliorate the stress of occupational low status. (See especially Crampton and Norton in the "Honeymooners" or Archie Bunker in "All In The Family").

A likely source of role inducing strain toward deviance is in what has been referred to as role engulfment or role encapsulation. One or a few roles that monopolize behavior are bound to be disabling. Role compatibility is the extent of stress between various roles. If there is role consistence, stress is reduced; if there is role primacy, where one dominates all others, stress is increased. Schur (1971: 69-71) describes role engulfment as the instance where one role dominates all others and thus dominates the personality. Sagarin (1975: 145) describes role encapsulation as the instance where one may be unable to escape from a status because it is too well liked or the person thinks escape is impossible. One may become encapsulated into a deviant role. Fixating on any role may be hazardous to mental and social health. The idea of engulfment or encapsulation is different from role specialization. This latter role-playing scenario involves limited choices within a range of acceptable behavior and is efficient and economical. Interaction can succeed with reduced energy (and ego) expenditure.

Role as a concept has been described along with its pertinence for deviance/conformity. A number of potential sources of strain toward conformity/deviance within the social structure as expressed by roles were also discussed above. Some of these are: the number of roles in a person's repertoire, role conflict, and role-taking skills. A number of these variables overlap such as role performance and role strain. In order to measure the contribution of role to conformity/deviance, a few of the dimensions of role can be translated into variables, assessed and then combined into an Index of Role Sufficiency. (See figure 4.1). The role variables could be: role numbers – using an instrument similar to an Adjective Check List the repertoire of roles would be explored to determine its poverty or richness; role conflict – can be assessed with a version of the Stauffer-Toby Conflict Scale (Stauffer and Toby, 1951); role-taking skill – sociopathic scale from Gough's CPI would be a useful measure; role-engulfment – a scale would need to be devised to determine the degree of balance among a person's various roles. The assessment of the various aspects of role should be diversely distributed among the salient social institutions. Once each variable is assessed, they can be combined into an Index of Role Sufficiency and linked to the deviance model.

Status

Reiterating from the previous section, role and status are two sides of the same coin. As such, much that is said about role would hold for status. But in the abstract, it possesses its own meaning, and as usual, it has complexity, differing definitions, ambiguity, and can be operationalized and included in the deviance model.

FIGURE 4.1

INDEX OF ROLE SUFFICIENCY

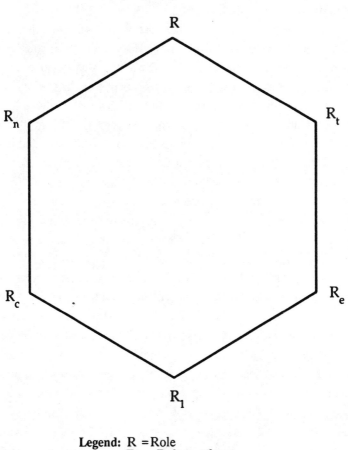

Legend: R =Role
R_n =Role numbers
R_c =Role conflict
R_t =Role taking
R_e =Role engulfment
R_1 =Role Sufficiency Index

Concern with inequality of manifold kinds has caught the attention of many early as well as contemporary thinkers.[2] Plato envisioned a class-

---

[2]For a history of different canceptions of social calss see Ossowski (1963).

structured society encompassing Guardians, Auxiliaries, and Workers. Aristotle in *Politics* envisioned three elements in all states: the very rich, very poor, and a mean. He opted for the mean as the best condition of life and as a source of rationality. St. Thomas, St. Augustine, Machiavelli, Hobbes, Locke, Burke, Bentham, Rousseau, and Hegel all evinced similar concerns but with different principles. Kant declared inequality as a source of both good and evil. The impulse for modern concerns probably came from Marx who averred that the history of all societies was one of class struggles. Most contemporary sociological analysis about stratification combine Marx and Weber, influencing such writers as Robert Lynd, W. Lloyd Warner, C. Wright Mills, Talcott Parsons, Lewis Coser, and Ralf Dahrendorf. The breadth of contemporary concern is with some version of social class and the distribution of the attributes that define the strata. For the theory of deviance as developed here, the major concern is less with stratification and more with status, less on equality and its sources and more on the consequences of the multifarious positions we assume or have imposed upon us for deviance/conformity.

Pareto (1935) declared, "History is a graveyard of aristocracies." This is drawn from his notion of the "circulation of elites." Though since discredited, the idea of an elite, in a modified version, and their circulation, might have some currency.[3] Belief systems change and with it the value carriers, those who gain power on some basis – economic, technological, moral, political – and manifest high status. But more often, domination is shared and transitory in the pluralistic society. Elites are not a class but an aggregate that share the attributes of contemporary and temporary criteria for status and do not share a consciousness or sense of common membership.

The ideas of Max Weber (1958) dominate studies of social class in America. He emphasized the difference between economic class, political authority and honor – class, party, and status. For Weber there are three separate dimensions of stratification systems: class, status and party, each required to understand such system because they vary independently (leading to problems of inconsistency), and the relative importance of each varies

---

[3]See Mills (1956) for an assessment of such elites as the political, military, industrial, and labor.

widely within and between societies. Class is based upon market conditions; status (stand) is an estimate of honor (Bendix, 1960: 104-106). A social class is people sharing some economic interests; a status group is people sharing honor or prestige (through such categories as ancestry, religion, and life style). Class is a number of people sharing one or more causes of life chances. This includes supply of goods, external living conditions, and personal life experiences. One life chance (e.g. wealth) could lead to another (e.g. higher education). Life styles refers to the evaluation of characteristics of status groups. The evaluation of a style of life determines its prestige. Those with power may be able to determine the social definition of a "proper style of life" and thus control status designations. Party, according to Weber, "lives in a house of power." Its action is directed toward influencing communal action.

Apparently stratification systems are universal. Veblen's analysis of conspicuous consumption implied a way to enhance status – and it occurs from the potlatch to the Cadillac. Simmel (Wolff, 1950) suggested three typical forms of subordination: an individual, a plurality, an impersonal objective principle. Sorokin (1959) refers to a social space as a universe of the human population. He continues by identifying social positions in this universe and its diverse aspects through concepts of horizontal and vertical dimensions. All Roman Catholics reflect the horizontal dimension while the difference between the Pope and priest, the vertical dimension.

The modern emphasis on status (as well as role) is usually attributed to Linton (1945). He conceived each status (position) with a single associated role. Merton (1957: 380-384) elaborated this concept by introducing the idea that each status involves an array of roles – a role-set. Then each person occupies many statuses, each with its own role-set. Merton calls these statuses a status-set – " a complex of distinctive positions." Status-sets provide one form of interdependence between institutions and subsystems of a society. There is considerable diversity in the complexity of each person's status-set and sometimes there is difficulty in articulating the status-set. Status generalization has been known and studied since the early days of sociology. It involves the process in which statuses, regardless of pertinence, intervene in an interaction by producing expectations often with significant consequences.

Why is stratification typical of modern societies? There are two important views that address this question – those of Marx and Lenski. Marx's view links power with those who own or control the means of production. Lenski (1966) suggests that an elite takes over or creates a new stratification system. The elite controls strategies that induce reciprocal reactions by nonelites. These reciprocal reactions take four major forms: competitive struggle, dropping out, petty thievery, the acquisition of technical expertise. These strategies of the nonelite groups explain, to a great extent, the characteristics of the social class systems of industrialized societies. Davis and Moore (1945) attempted to answer the same question with another approach. They expounded the functional necessity of stratification. Stratification is indispensable to the maintenance of the social structure – an approach which was met with considerable criticism and diminishing influence.

Status contains and incorporates many complexities. As the concept expanded, it gained intricacy. Nisbet (1970: 182) stated that "Hierarchy, stratification, and rank are the very essence of status." He described it as a way of behavior, part of a social circle (alluding to its interdependence), bounded and reinforced by norms, including an element of legitimacy, and containing a sense of obligation and duty. These are the criteria for status.

Class and status are not synonymous, though elements of each overlap. The tendency is to consider status within the context of the social aggregate called class or caste and to study it as social stratification. Parsons (1954: 75-76) asserts that status, in a system of stratification, is attributed to the evaluation of each of six aspects: membership in a kinship unit, personal qualities, achievements, possessions, authority, power. But it is obvious that there are all kinds of status relationships outside of class, especially in a complex society. There is a profusion of social levels, statuses, interest groups, associations, elites, political electorates, all vying for dominance. Status rather than class may be the core concept in stratification. Nisbet (1970: 208) distinguishes between class and level. The difference is in the element of consciousness. Class consciousness is a group awareness; level consciousness is a high degree of individual awareness – a sentience of one's own level which can act as an impetus for upper mobility. The awareness of one's level becomes a driving force for change. Status has a double meaning. In the abstract it is a position in a particular pattern. Thus each one has many statuses. However, if not qualified (e.g. economic status) it can refer to the sum total of all statuses like in a social class. A status system involves organized statuses, inclined toward hierarchy and evaluation, such as in social class. Many statuses are used to designate a position in a system of ranking such as in social class. But others do not connote a higher or lower position in a significant way like mother or friend. Class implies material rewards; status implies symbolic rewards. Though different they are prone to coincide.

The components of status are considerable. Status applies to a person or a collectivity. Each society has its own differentiation or esteem ranking and rewards – regardless of dedication to equality. The same high or low prestige assigned to a given status is not universally accorded. In most cases it is consensual; in some cases, limited. At times the prestige is directed toward the position, at other times, toward the person in the position, and at best to both. The President of the United States has high prestige, yet to many President Nixon had little. A medical doctor holds a high status, but as a person, he may be denigrated.

In many instances one can rise above or fall below expectations and status will follow, depending on the person's capacity for status. Some women receive more status than most other women; a rich person may lose the prestige associated with wealth. Some statuses are unstable or temporary or false. A triad may be temporary, a student may hold a seasonal job, an imposter may make an unjustified claim of wealth. Each person enters an interaction with an identity, a position, or status. Sometimes the status is false or misinterpreted which in either case contributes to the definition of the situation. There are those who assume inappropriate statuses. Mechanisms emerge to level the misplaced status. A demand for high status may be leveled through ridicule. Some people disguise their status or the status may come from disguising it. The person who buys drinks at a bar for all may seek status of wealth without money. A person may drive a small junky car and wear old sneakers in spite of wealth.

Some argue the imputation of a moral component in superior-inferior designations (Douglas 1970: 6-8; Parsons 1954: 69-88). Higher status implies, in the abstract, higher virtue. Others argue the inclusion of the element of legitimacy. Without it, the particular status would wither away. There is hierarchy among statuses. High occupation can be effected by low race – the lawyer has his status diluted by being black. Status can become a goal, a preoccupation with desires, apprehensions, anxieties, deviance – a motivator of action. In addition to the obvious differences between people (age, gender, race,), differentiation can occur according to regularly performed patterns of activity.

Shils (1970: 420-448) equates deference with status. Each interaction involves an element of appreciation or derogation in assorted degrees. It is these acts of appreciation or derogation that Shils refers to as deference. Socioeconomic status is a sum total status; status as deference has an evaluative dimension. Deference may be expected but not received or received when not expected. A stylish crook may get deference from his subcultures but derogation outside of it. The opposite is also possible. Shils believes that western societies are moving toward deference indifference. Equals in contemporary society seem to lose the ritual of deference. Deference entitlements include: occupation, role and accomplishment, wealth, income and the way it is acquired, style of life, level of education, political or corporate power, kinship connections, ethnicity, performance for community or society, titles or ranks. On the basis of these entitlements people regulate their behavior and anticipate deferential or derogatory responses. The properties described as deference entitlements are significant because of the charisma attached to them (Shils 1970: 423). The charisma indicates society's attachment of significance.

There are many reasons people raise claims for prestige and others honor the claim. The claims include such factors as: property, birth, occupation, education, income, power, or as Mills (1951: 239) notes, "...anything that may invidiously distinguish one person from another." The extent of claims and those who honor them vary widely. The claim may have many hierarchies of prestige. Some claims are almost universally accepted, others almost universally rejected. In general, according to Mills, there is ambivalence in the claims to prestige and the honoring of these claims. The ambivalence subjects the system to such great stress as to put people in a "virtual status panic."

Statuses are bound and reinforced by norms; they are acquired by socialization. Over a life-span, each person is exposed to and acquires new statuses. Conventionally, two types of status are recognized; ascribed status and achieved status. The former is those assigned without reference to innate differences or abilities. The latter is filled by effort, competition, talent. A large number are parcelled out on the basis of gender, age, and family relationships (ascribed). There are other paths to status including maturation (vote at 21), creation (fatherhood or motherhood), (Tumin 1967: 47). Societies have a coalescence of these sources though one or more are apt to dominate. A change of status could be integrating (marriage) or disintegrating (unemployment). statuses are interdependent. The patriarch of a family is inseparable from those below him in the family. His status is high because theirs is low; theirs is low because his is high. Linton (1945: 78-130) distinguishes active status from latent status. The former is a position one is operating in at one point in time. The latter is the other status, for the time being. Linton also suggests a status personality – reponses linked to a status configuration – for example, gender, social class, age. Short (1964: 120) offers the idea of "status management" where behavior is directed to achieving some desired position or sustaining a position already achieved.

Dahrendorf (1970: 6) asserts that inequalities can be distinguished in two respects. First, there are inequalities of natural talent and social position. Second, there are inequalities that involve evaluative rank order and those that do not. From these assumptions Dahrendorf postulates four types of inequality:

1. Natural differences of kind – features, characters, interests.
2. Natural differences of rank – intelligence, talent, strength.
3. Social differentiation of positions about equal in rank.
4. Social stratification based on reputation and wealth and ranked by social status.

Goffman (1983: 14) identifies four critical statuses: age grade, gender, class, and race. They represent almost infallible ways to categorically identify a person, an identification that introduces critical data into a social interaction. Homans (1961) states that anything that distinguishes one individual from another is a status factor. It could include skin color, age, religion, income, skills, personal appearance, and many others. The status of the same individual might be congruent in relation to some people yet incongruent in relation to others. Linton (1936), who introduced the concepts of ascribed and achieved statuses (as well as role), identified the salient ones as age, sex, family relationships, and caste or class. Tumin (1967: 20-21) suggests that statuses can be ranked on the basis of three criteria: personal characteristics, trained skills, and abilities. He also notes three general types of rewards in statuses: property, power, and psychic gratification.

Attributes and the lack of them are translated into inequalities in wealth, power, status, opportunity. Social institutions have their own form of stratification. The economic sphere has wealth; politics, power; religion, morality; family, gender; occupation, prestige. The criteria for status are diverse and not universal for all statuses. Some are operative at some time for many people – gender, age, wealth, political authority, ethnicity, education, occupation, kinship groups. The criteria for evaluating status approaches infinity. Some of those most frequently employed include: beauty, courage, holiness, cleanliness, age, gender, ethnicity, kinship, nobility, power, skill, intelligence, strength, learning, morality, (Tumin, 1967: 32). These are personal qualities. There are also other qualities. There are functions requiring performance to maintain society such as educating children, dealing with illness, preserving law and order. Once a status is secured, it needs to be validated by fulfilling the role requirements. Opportunity structure can be reflected in the assessment of status role – social status embodies opportunity structure which helps determine the distribution of deviance.

The more one contemplates status, the more facets emerge. Becker (1963: 31-34) postulates a master status. This idea is similar to that of role encapsulation. The criminal as a master status would dominate the perceptions and interactions of the repetitive amateur as well as the professional. What does the thief "see" when he enters a bank or supermarket? Status determines social identity. It is a salient feature of social life. A master status is bound to dominate a self-perception and social identity. With a master status or without one, other positions assume some form of hierarchy. Is there a consensual hierarchy of status? Which is more significant, ascribed or achieved, primary or secondary, formal or informal, personal or social? Shibutani (1961: 419-425) avers that the loss of personal face is more significant than loss of social position.

Status influences social responses. The status of the family, other groups, self, effects experiences and relationships. The consequences are probably hardest on males, the young, and minorities. One consequence could be frustration. Status frustration as related to delinquency was popularized by Albert Cohen (1955). Status frustration was viewed as eliciting deviant responses (see also Finestone 1957). In the status universe we measure ourselves according to middle class criteria. Crime and delinquency become reactions to difficulty in achieving status in the legitimate structure. However, critical assessment has questioned the significance of status frustration for crime and delinquency. Another consequence might be anomia. Bell (1957) asserted that anomia is more prevalent in the lower than in the upper end of the social strata.

Status is a source of conflict and stress. Individuals subjected to conflicting status obligations might find themselves under considerable stress. The more complex the status-sets, the more exposure to potential stress. Status conflicts are distinguished from class conflicts. The latter are economically oriented while the former are prestige or honor oriented (see Gusfield 1975: 222-240). Gibbs and Martin (1958) argue that the number of status-sets occupied is related to the amount of role conflict of the status-sets. Role conflict increases as the extent of status occupancy decreases. The fewer people in a status, the greater the role conflict. Women airline pilots, doctors, engineers, have greater role conflict than men airline pilots, doctors, engineers (Rushing 1969).

The consequences can be tempered by the ability to adapt and cope. This ability is enhanced by the "others" in an interaction in their willingness to actuate such traits as empathy. Furthermore, normative patterns emerge to cushion the conflicts such as a hierarchy of obligations. Merton (1957:

382) suggests status-sequences as a mechanism to reduce conflict. This is the succession of statuses one moves through. This involves a process of self-selection which would have a higher probability of producing stress. Thus one tends to achieve statuses consistent with existing values.

How does status effect deviance? Among other things, it serves as a motivator, as a source of stress, identity, and sense of self worth. Esteem grows as performance levels rise. One cost of deviant acts is disesteem. Higher status people receive more esteem and disesteem for the same performance levels than lower status people (Erickson and Nosanchuk 1984). Laws proclaiming predatory acts as criminal can be initiated by class interest groups while laws embodying non-predatory acts are prone to be initiated by moral entrepreneurs who represent status groups that feel threatened by other life styles (Glaser, 1978: 22-23). Status, as a correlate of deviance, is well documented but still moot. At first it was thought to be highly correlated, then thought to be unrelated, but then more evidence of a relationship surfaced (Thornberry and Farnworth 1982). Deviant vs. nondeviant comparisons indicate different attributes distinguishing low status from high status. From a labeling perspective mental illness is described as an ascriptive status (Scheff 1964). This could also hold for other forms of deviance. A deviant status usually is not transitory. The social reaction is institutionalized as in stigma. Deviance goes beyond the act. When the perception shifted from the act to the actor, deviant status shifted from transitory to permanency. The act remains deviant forever – even with ameliorating ceremonies. The social expectation is for a continuation of deviant acts which can become a self-fulfilling prophecy.

There is considerable literature on the concept of status inconsistency. If a person ranks high in one status but relatively low in one or more statuses it is referred to as status inconsistency. It has also been referred to as status crystallization or status congruence. It is alleged that inconsistency can be psychologically disturbing. However, there are different responses to different types of inconsistencies (Jackson 1962). In some cases the responses can manage the effect of the inconsistencies. Several studies have shown a relationship between status inconsistency and such factors as: suicide, prejudice, voting patterns, social isolation, mobility striving, social mobility, political liberalism, psychosomatic symptoms of stress, and preference for or attempts to change the social order (Lenski 1954, 1956; Jackson 1962).

As analysis proceeded the complexity increased. Geschwender (1970: 508) suggested that the consequences of status inconsistency could be explained within the framework of an expanded version of dissonance theory. Wiley (1963: 156-157) offered two varieties of status inconsistency: positional and reputational. Positional inconsistency involves a high position in one status dimension (e.g. income) and a low position in another dimension (e.g. education). Reputational inconsistency involves different degrees of honor from different community segments. For example, this might include attribution of high status for a wealthy person from the working class but less status for a wealthy person from the upper class. A theory of social certitude was developed (Zaleznik, et al. 1958: 55-56). This theory assumes that each status position has a set of behavioral expectations regarding behavior of ego and all interacting alter-egos. A status consistent person has sets of behavioral expectations which reinforce or are consistent with one another. Therefore a condition of social certitude exists and social relations are harmonious. The status inconsistent has sets of expectations in conflict. There is no social certitude and anxiety prevails as social relations are unsatisfactory. This lack of social certitude sets in motion forces that attempt to create status consistency. This theory broadens the process of consistency/inconsistency beyond a static notion of two or more statuses with varying degrees of honor or prestige. One writer suggests two possible consequences of status inconsistency (Runciman, 1970: 176-177). First, the person will try to bring all ranks into equilibrium by raising lower rank. Second, the person will deny the validity of criteria which assign him lower rank. Until he succeeds, psychological stress remains.

The relationship between stress and status inconsistency is not a simple linear one. Sometimes inconsistency is a deliberate choice to ameliorate or manage stress but at a lower level of status. Status inconsistency research tends to be static in that it does not deal with actors' interaction with the inconsistency. One can argue that inconsistency can be a buffer against strain as well as a contributor to it. A compensatory view of inconsistency focuses on the personality as a great ameliorator of stress and strain. Just as status inconsistency can be positive for the low status person through high status position in certain areas (e.g. a voluntary organization or the family), it can be positive for the high status person who takes out the garbage at home or is an abominable golfer or tennis player at the country club. In this leveling process, the low status person has his uplifting moments while the high status person has his moments of humility. It is too often assumed that stress induced by status inconsistency leads to negative consequences. There is a readiness to neglect the individual's ability to temper or manage the inconsistency as one would manage a spoiled identity (see Hornung 1977).

The impact of status on conformity/deviance can be measured by its components. Some measure of "structural acculturation" would assess the impact of status on behavior. Status can be related normatively to the dominant culture. An adaption score can account for status contribution to deviance. It is not enough to be socially, ethnically, religiously, sexually, biologically, economically, chronologically different, but the accommodation can make the difference indifferent. Black or Hispanic, teen or adult, male or female, all adjust or do not adjust to the expectations of others (whether powerful or not). The adequacy of the adjustment determines the outcome of social control. What is the nature of the status and where is it sought – in a subculture, the dominant culture, or some kind of mix?

Rushing (1969) asserts that role conflict increases as the extent of status occupancy decreases. The fewer people in a status, the greater the role conflict. Furthermore, the number of statuses and the esteem or honor we think is attached to it can measure the contribution of status to conformity. Thus the sheer number of statuses and the number of unexpected people in a status can contribute to deviance/conformity.

Another measure of the effect of status on deviance/conformity is offered by Gibbs and Martin (1958). Conformity to roles of one status can interfere with those of another status. Gibbs and Martin postulate that the extent of incompatible statuses varies inversely with the degree of status integration. The measure of status integration involves identifying salient statuses (e.g. sex), dividing each into classes (e.g. male and female) and determining a configuration of statuses (i.e. two or more simultaneously occupied statuses). Gibbs and Martin assign scores, computed the sum of the squares (ΣX^2) of each status configuration. The greater the ΣX^2 the greater the status integration. The greater the integration, the less conflict and stress (Gibbs and Martin 1964). Adams (1953-1954) identified nine status factors (e.g. age, education) and constructed a score of status congruence. These scores were associated with degree of confidence for others in the group and degree of friendship with others.

The conflicting demands of two or more statuses could produce tensions with consequences for deviance. For example, religious and occupational statuses could play havoc with one's "nerves"; a religious fundamentalist with liberal attitudes in a social welfare occupation could be stressed by the abortion issue. Some measures of this dissonance or status stress would contribute to an Index of Status. Such a measure is different from status inconsistency as it would involve status-consistent persons with opposites in obligations and expectations but not in position. Status consistency could be measured separately but with allowances for the value of a compensatory status. Such an Index of Status Consistency would include an assessment of a person's management of "status structure."

There is a host of dimensions in the measurement of status. What role does status consciousness play? One would expect that the higher the consciousness of status–especially when connected to success and failure–the higher the degree of stress. Consciousness induces anxiety; ignorance is bliss. People may claim status (rightfully or not) and the claim can be honored or rejected. These claims and their acceptance or rejection can be assessed and compiled into a Status Acceptance Score.

The Capacity for Status (CS) Scale of the California Psychological Inventory (CPI) measures a capacity for status. It is a score of the capacity or receptiveness for status and not an actual status. It measures personal qualities which underlie and lead to status. Such scores are significant in interpreting profiles of deviants. There are many personal qualities frequently used as criteria in evaluating status (e.g. beauty, courage, cleanliness). A device like an Adjective Check List could be used to assess one's perception of possession of these qualities coupled with one's perception of another's perception of one's possession of these qualities. This would permit an evaluation of a capacity for status based upon personal qualities as well as the perception of a reception of these claims by others. A social status scale could be developed when one places oneself on a status scale relative to others and where one places oneself on a status scale relative to others and where one thinks these others believe that person belongs on the scale. This could identify a person's perception of a status self and the degree to which it is honored. Several variables of this nature (e.g. the CS Scale) might be developed into a status profile as a graphic measure of one's status.

Previous work has indicated the significance of status for deviance/conformity. A number of possible measures of status in its various manifestations are noted above. They include:

1. Status Adaptation Score
2. Status Occupancy Score
3. Status Integration Score
4. Status Stress Score
5. Status Consistency Score
6. Status consciousness Score
7. Status Acceptance Score
8. Capacity For Status Score
9. Capacity For Status Through Personal Qualities Score
10. Social Status Scale
11. Status Profile

From this universe of variables four relevant scores are selected to form a Status Stability Index: Status Adaptation Score, Status Occupancy Score, Status Consistency Score, Capacity For Status Score. (See Figure 4.2). The contribution of this Index to conformity/deviance can then be related to the deviance model.

Associations

Associations generate strains with deviant consequences. The same system generates control with conforming consequences. When these two strains are in equilibrium, deviance still occurs – perhaps in a normative pattern, as Durkheim suggests. Therefore, they are included in the deviance model. There is an inclination to abstract deviance phenomena as an independent entity. This limits theory and misses the intricate nature of the deviant process. This applies when the abstraction is from structure in the form of social institutions, but becomes accreted when linked to structure, structure to culture, and both to personality. Structure, culture, and personality describe; process explains.

FIGURE 4.2

INDEX OF STATUS STABILITY

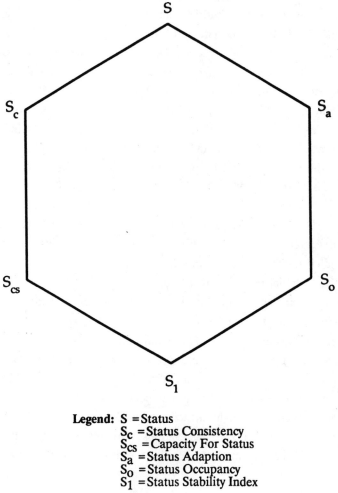

Legend: S = Status
Sc = Status Consistency
Scs = Capacity For Status
Sa = Status Adaption
So = Status Occupancy
S1 = Status Stability Index

There are recurring problems requiring standardized solutions for social existence. Some of these functional imperatives are reproduction, property, exchange, role differentiation, health, and socialization. These needs are met through social institutions–with varying degrees of success. There are several ways to describe and define social institutions–some more dynamic than others and in either case, considered inadequate. Generally, the idea is that special purpose organizations (e.g. trade unions) are associations. When an association serves a public interest (e.g. government) it is an institution. An institution is an association that is highly organized, systematized and stable. Bierstedt (1974: 328-329) states that an association is any organized group with structure, continuity, an identity, and a name; an institution is not a group but an organized procedure, formal and established, pursuing some activity in society. In his introduction to the *Unadjusted Girl*, W.I. Thomas noted that the fundamental function of institutions was to "define the situation" for action. Sumner's Folkways (1960) insists that institutions consist of an idea and structure. It begins in folkways, becomes custom, develops into mores, produces a structure, and emerges as an institution. Parsons (1954: 231-232) defines institutions as a legitimized system of patterned expectations. The key to this definition is in the concept of roles. The patterns define the roles of the participating actors. Parsons postulates three classes of institutions: situational, e.g. kinship; instrumental, e.g. medicine; integrative, e.g. stratification.

Institutional patterns are the basic elements of a social system and therefore require integration for stability. Theoretically, institutions are at odds with one another and can become the breeding ground for system deviance. This is analogous to Durkheim's idea of anomie. Norms govern roles and roles govern institutions. A breakdown of either (probably both) increases the risk of deviant outbreaks. Institutions act as maintenance machinery; in essence they "keep the peace." The institutional structure provides for control through corrective, retaliatory, and punitive measures. To a large extent, control by associations, particularly institutions, extrude from its structural form–bureaucratic–the boon and bane of western society.

The list of associations is substantial. It includes: political, economic, and religious institutions, the family, voluntary associations, and some theorists would add public opinion and the mass media. They all involve formal and informal control. Secondary groups utilize informal mechanisms such as ridicule, warnings, safe places, and ostracism; they also use such formal mechanisms as termination of employment, promises of success, entertainment, and recourse. Voluntary associations compromise a mosaic of organizations including Elks, DAR, Boy Scouts, Chamber of Commerce, Kiwanis, and WCTU. They cover secret societies, clubs, recreation teams, art groups, mutual aid societies, lodges and many other. They all link participants to a larger network of social relationships with exposure to social control. The activity is usually normative with negotiation and compromise as well as control.

Associations provide a normative structure specifying conforming behavior with rewards and punishments. The degree of success in controlling behavior, to a great extent, depends upon the number of impactful associations, whether they are definitive and strong rather than diffuse and weak, and such mechanisms as sanctuary. Departure from an integrated nuclear family can adversely effect social behavior. A sense of community assessed by common interests, sharing, a willingness to take sanctioning action can reduce deviance. If the individual is concerned about what church, neighbors, parents, employers, think about his behavior, conformity is more likely to ensue (see Jessor, et. al. 1968: 74-77). Social isolation limits effective control–a clue to the measurement of effective social control. Yet one study suggested that the relationship between delinquency and attachment to school was reciprocal rather than recursive; delinquency was as much a cause as a consequence of school attachment (Liska and Reed, 1985).

Not all associations are equally immersed in social control activities nor equally effective. Those associated with criminal justice and family are closer to social control than school, church, mass media, and others. A hierarchy of associations relative to community success with social control is highly likely. The hierarchy would vary somewhat from community to community as would the total institutional or associational impact on deviance/control. Any evaluation would require a weighting factor to measure the differential impacts.

For the model of deviance the broader notion association is adopted and three specific aspects explored: association bonds, coping mechanisms, and association reaction (visibility, tolerance, stigma). (See Figure 4.3).

FIGURE 4.3

INDEX OF ASSOCIATIONAL EFFECTIVENESS

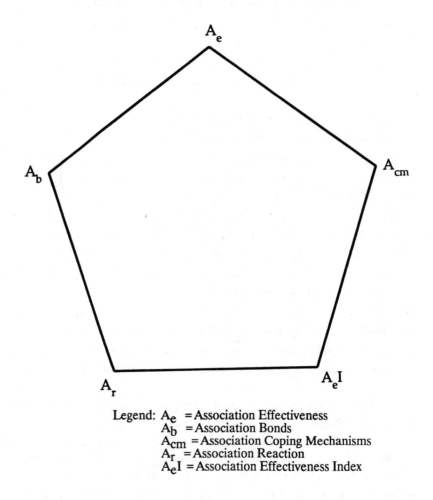

Legend: A_e = Association Effectiveness
A_b = Association Bonds
A_{cm} = Association Coping Mechanisms
A_r = Association Reaction
$A_e I$ = Association Effectiveness Index

Association Bonds – If associations function as peace maintaining machinery, with varying degrees of effectiveness, it should follow that the contribution to control is enhanced by two factors. First, the larger the number of associations to which one belongs, the more apt one is to conform. Second, the stronger the bond to an association the more conforming the participant. Combining the two factors should permit a measure of the effectiveness of associations for conformity/deviance. This can be achieved by linking the number of associations one belongs to with the additional query regarding the degree of attachment to each of the associations. This Index of Association Bond score would be included in an Index of Association Effectiveness.

Coping Mechanisms – All aspects of a social system develop and employ coping mechanisms. These means of alleviating strain contribute to harmony and conformity. Associations manifest a number of such means unique to their particular structure. There is considerable redundancy in the concepts of association and culture and their mechanisms of social control. This reflects the fragile nature of the concepts themselves. Much that was noted in a previous section on cultural copings applies as well in association copings. Some mechanisms are more identifiable with associations than with culture and can be used to contribute to an index of the effectiveness of associations in controlling behavior.

There are a considerable number of associations. Many are institutions with clear-cut functions fairly easy to describe but more difficult to justify in the form in which they operate. Associations include assorted economic institutions, disparate religious institutions, diverse administration of justice machinery, government, education, family, university, corporation, trade union, and a host of voluntary associations – clubs, lodges, scouts, teams, professional organizations, esthetic groups (art, music, drama), ethnic formations, chambers of commerce, and many others. From this torrent of associations one can choose a number of significant ones to assess the effect of the coping mechanisms. Three major ones are suggested: family, administration of justice, and voluntary associations.

The family is clearly the cardinal institution in the social system. Coping is a fundamental aspect of the family. Considering the intimacy, the quantity of interaction, it is bound to be a well spring of stress, strain, frustration, and the whole gamut of emotions. Yet it survives, and when it fails, it is regularly sought again. Close analysis shows that the family tolerates from its members the consequences of interaction which it would readily object to, repel, and retaliate against from any other source. The family offers sanctuary from the abrasiveness of the rest of the system, and opportunity to manage tension and stigma, a safe place to adopt roles prohibited or limited elsewhere, and the feared sanction of ostracism. These mechanisms maintain harmony, relieve tension, and offer a haven from the "cruelties" of other associations. Of course, as the preeminent group it can also produce stress and misbehavior. Thus as a significant factor in control and deviance, it is an important source for measuring the direction its potential will go. The effectiveness of coping mechanisms become an essential element in any measure of institutional effectiveness for conformity/deviance.

The most obvious of the institutions for social control are the manifold organizations dedicated to the administration of justice – particularly law enforcement agencies. Not only is the manifest enforcement and adjudication of rules significant, but also the latent controlling processes. That is, is the adjudication process and enforcement process pursued vigorously or practiced with indifference? Each community presents a will to control ranging from weak to strong – one that is perceived by the participants, with repercussions for conformity/deviance. There is a rich vein of writings extolling or criticizing the system of justice and its outcome. One key aspect of their operations is the nature of the activity among which the proactive vs. reactive concepts are important.

Regardless of the operations, there are an assortment of coping mechanisms available which effect the goal of control. It is not all pursuit, apprehension, and retribution. In many instances they serve as dispute arbitrators – particularly the police on the beat and the judge in chambers. These conditions relieve stress and effect control. Other coping mechanisms include role suspension where controlled misbehavior is permitted or coopted; legal recourse permitting a person to challenge the system and offer respite from over-control; legal fictions like name changes and adoptions to resolve sources of tension; and system activity, the diverse ways in which the agencies pursue their legitimate goals. The extent of the effectiveness of the mechanisms are measurable either by assessing the institution itself or the community's perception of the institution. A score could be devised that measures the leverage of the coping mechanisms and then the score can be included in the evaluation of the institutional contribution to conformity/deviance.

Americans are a nation of joiners, a striking feature not lost on the observant Alexis de Tocqueville. Some estimates indicate more than 100,000 voluntary associations in United States. Most Americans join one or more voluntary associations; there must be considerable benefits to counteract the costs. The benefit might fulfill some specific need or solve some group problem. Nevertheless it serves as an arena for both formal and informal interaction with primary as well as secondary relationships, coalescing with import for behavior.

The associations do provide mechanisms to cope with stress especially of urban life. Rules are often redefined and roles dissipated. Statuses can be liberated so that different rules apply; demeanor can be relaxed and new norms imposed. The low status person with insignificant roles can gain position and esteem beyond what is possible elsewhere. The janitor becomes captain of the bowling team; the unemployed, the head Moose; the insignificant, significant. Nonnormative roles can be legitimized, pent-up energy dissipated, and propaganda offered to serve egos. These assorted mechanisms relieve stress, offer yearned for esteem, and create a haven for mediocrity and failure.

A number of mechanisms can be identified, evaluated for effectiveness, and included in the measure of association contributions to conformity/deviance. The mechanisms could include: rule redefinition, propaganda, energy displacement, nonnormative role legitimation, and role dissipation. (See table 4.1).

TABLE 4.1

SOME ASSOCIATIONAL COPING MECHANISMS

	FAMILY	ADMINISTRATION OF JUSTICE	VOLUNTARY ASSOCIATIONS
C	tension management	dispute arbitration	rule redefinition
O P	sanctuary	rule suspension	propoganda
I	stigma management	legal recourse	role dissipation
N G	safe place	legal fictions	energy desplacement
S	ostracism	system activity-inertia-vigor	legitimate non-normative roles

The combined score, would be used to calculate the Association Effectiveness Index, (Figure 4.3).

Association Reactions – Although previously considered, the social reaction to deviance and its consequences was popularized by the labelling approach (Kitsuse, 1964; Erikson, 1962; Becker, 1963; Lemert, 1967). As Erikson aptly noted, "Deviance is not a property inherent in certain forms of behavior, it is a property conferred upon these forms by the audiences which directly or indirectly witness them," (Erikson, 1962: 308). A torrent of literature flowed from this premise substantiating the considerable impact of social reaction to the deviance process. However, heavily criticized (as every theory has been) this focus has subsided, although its importance for deviance remains. Audience reaction may not explain deviance but it does contribute something to the explanation. The reaction to behavior (and misbehavior) initiates the controlling function of associations. The action is perceived (visibility), is reacted to (tolerance), and is labelled (stigma). These three aspects of the reaction process overlap and are interdependent. It is not a simple linear process but one of great complexity with a multitude of intervening variables. However, these aspects of social reaction can be evaluated and serve as an indice of associations' contribution to conformity/deviance. (See Figure 4.4).

FIGURE 4.4

ASSOCIATION REACTION TO ACTION INDEX

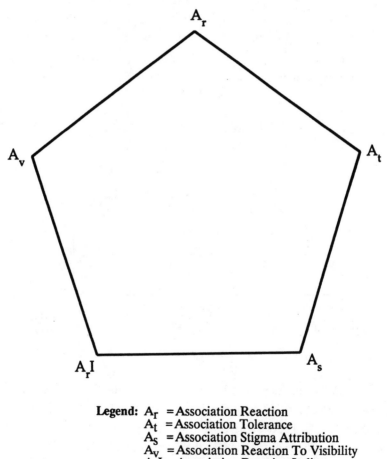

Legend: A_r = Association Reaction
A_t = Association Tolerance
A_s = Association Stigma Attribution
A_v = Association Reaction To Visibility
A_rI = Association Reaction Indice

As noted, social reaction to behavior or misbehavior is linked to the visibility of behavior and its judgment, the tolerance or rejection of the act(s) and/or the actor(s). Of course there are conditions in which an act may be rejected but not stigmatized; the visibility may be perceived negatively but still tolerated; the visibility may be perceived negatively, rejected, but not stigmatized. Similar combinations show that the outcome is not linear and inevitable. There are contingent conditions under which the process is interrupted or cancelled. It may include such contigent conditions as social class, age, gender, and many others. Evaluating the outcome would then require three alternatives (or quantification along a continuum); one in which the outcome is positive, one in which the outcome is negative, and one in which it is ambiguous, but leaning toward a negative outcome – that is, the actor is flirting with negative consequences. (See Figure 4.5).

FIGURE 4.5

ASSOCIATION REACTION TO ACTION

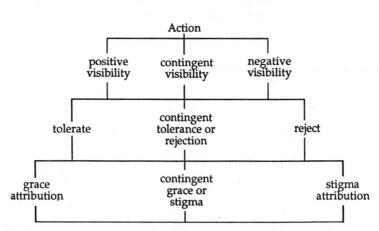

Visibility – In identifying a criminal, must the act be perceived or known to others, specifically the justice system? This question has been posed often. To know or perceive a deviant act is part of the concept of visibility. Another aspect involves the perception of deviant potential – the potential in the eye of the beholder. Perception of potential can range from long hair to fingerprints at the scene of a crime. The black Rastafarian was repeatedly arrested because he looked dangerous. This question of visibility has received minor attention in the literature, perhaps except for labelling theorists. The major focus of the model deviance conceived here is on the latent or potential consequences of visibility as seen by the far-ranging control system.

Merton (1957: 319-322) extends the idea of visibility to "social visibility" – the visibility of one's status identity. He defines it as "the extent to which norms and the role-performances within a group are readily open to observation by others" (Merton, 1957: 319). This property permits behavior to be monitored and to return deviance back to the normative (with limitations). Impediments to visibility can result in fitful application of social control, at times too late for effective informal mechanisms. The nature of the formal control network and the stealthiness of crime patterns in a community establishes the degree of visibility and the eventual control and prevention.

Lemert (1967) has noted that the deviant person's role, status, function and self-definition are effected by the amount of deviation he engages in, the degree of social visibility, and the social reaction. The visibility is a function of the audience. We see here the social reaction emphasis of the labelling approach. In a later article, Lemert (1974: 457) defined social tolerance as a number of processes by which societies react to deviance through informal and formal means. He linked the form and intensity of the reaction to the nature, degree, extent, and visibility of the deviance.

Inciardi (1978: 147-153) suggested that the degree of visibility was the primary determinant of societal reactions. He postulated three dimensions to social visibility: as seen by the victim, by society's control system, by society at large. One could add a fourth dimension, as seen by the deviant himself. Sagarin (1975: 279-294) relates visibility to various kinds of deviance: pretended deviance, secret deviance, invisible deviance, the falsely accused, the imposter, the unaware deviant.

Is the invisible deviant deviant? Labelling theory would say probably not. But if the definition goes beyond an audience and includes the deviant's anticipation of a social reaction, then the answer could become affirmative. After all, most deviants prefer and seek invisibility. If deviance is a social phenomena it would require visibility. The unknown miscreant and his intimate others is likely to be influenced by the errant behavior which in turn may lead to discovery. From a labelling perspective, deviance requires some visibility for societal reaction (Lemert, 1951, 51). Even outside the framework of labelling, deviance is a relative concept, differentially defined in time and place. If not inherent it requires social disapproval for a reaction and consequently must have some visibility. This does not mean that the visibility must involve formal organizations and sanctions, but that some social entity–family, friends(?), employer, neighborhood, and others–become aware, perhaps sanctions informally and identifies the person as deviant, as mild as the reproach may be.

If one distinguishes the act from the actor, the former may be identified as deviant (an assault), but the actor remains unknown. When the two are connected, the actor becomes a deviant. One aspect of visibility is created by the apprehension process. In some cases, an act is taken for granted and becomes deviant when it becomes visible, interpreted and reacted to by the public. For example, in certain communities cohabiting becomes adultery or homosexuality (Sagarin, 1975: 279-294). Visibility goes beyond the "smoking gun." Some people advertise a deviant potential with personal demeanor and dress, bumper stickers, motorcycles, hang-outs, tattoos, and speeding in stolen cars (Heussenstamm, 1971). Several studies ٫٫ mental illness show a denial of visibility or a high tolerance by the family for deviant behavior as some factors which blind the perceiver (Goffman, 1959; Sampson, et. al. 1962).

Visibility is a process that ego can begin imperceptibly and then efface yet be seen and remembered by an audience; it can be gross and traumatic yet be invisible and veiled by an audience. It can circumscribe a significant part of society that can and does shape a response, not just ego, an accomplice or a gang, that ignores, hides, orthis is an appropriate idea) glorifies it. It includes the "dramatization of evil" and labelling as well as a smoking gun; it is linked to social tolerance which can confer ambiguity and selectiveness. It feeds on bias and power–blacks, hippies, homosexuals, teenagers, long hair, and unkept beards which evoke an anticipation of deviance. In defining the situation, different perspectives occur between ego and audience and within the audience itself. It is the first step in the labelling process and in the identification as deviant. Visibility is the observation or anticipation of an act either directly as a witness or indirectly as reported, (Hawkins and Tiedman, 1975). Nevertheless most rule breaking is not detected (see Erikson and Empey, 1963).

Visibility is a complex process that extends beyond the act. It is markedly limited if the behavior occurs in private. Public behavior is more apt to be observed while private behavior is more apt to be reported. Nevertheless, some private places are more public than public ones (parties at home, cars); some public places are more private than private places (elevators, hallways in public housing). Certain people live a more public life. Urban poor are more apt to be in the streets than those from the middle and upper classes. Higher status can reduce social visibility as it is easier to cover-up one's activities. Many people have more contact with public bureaucracies and are more visible as a result. Visibility is diminished by physical and social isolation – wihdrawal within the home, alcoholism, residence in the mountains and deserts, protection or isolation by parents and friends. On the other hand, technology, with its cameras and computers has increased visibility. Certain crimes are more visible than others – burglary and auto theft use stealth and caution, assault and robbery uses visibility bolstered by aggression. Use of certain bumper stickers, argot, long hair, inappropriate dress, attendance at suspect meetings, all increase visibility and invite intolerance and formal or informal control. The nature of the observer influences visibility. Some people are trained to search for deviance (police, psychiatrist).

Many factors intrude into the visibility process effecting the degree of visibility and the reaction to it. The alleged degree of harm in the eye of the beholder can determine the reaction outcome of the behavior and this includes the definition of the situation, a factor with considerable variability. Visibility is heightened by the cumulative nature of justice. Once a deviant act is perceived, no matter how insignificant, repetition enhances visibility and aggravates the reaction. In an interesting study of minority visibility

Kephart (1954) found that as the number of blacks increase arithmetically, their visibility increases exponentially. If this idea can be extended, minor visible nonnormative acts that are tolerated can be rejected as the acts increase slightly and the perception of potential harm increases drastically. A few teenagers in a shopping mall are a nuisance, just a few more is a catastrophe. A few punk rockers in an area are a curiosity, a few more are a threat.

Visibility also applies to and serves organizational contributions to social control. In earlier times town criers and posting of proclamations and rules made palpable the expected norms and consequences of deviance. The media, open courts, marked police cars and uniformed police, and the evident presence of authority serves a contemporary similar purpose.

There are many attributes of visibility; a number are referred to above. An assessment of several of the variables can be combined into an index of visibility. These might include: symbols of alienation (argot, tattoos, hang-outs, dress); demeanor (does person try to stand out or fade into a public background); repetition (does person tend to repeat the faux pas, nonnormative act, errancy); associational invisibility (does person perceive organizational authority as weak stupid, fallible, look at it with incredulity, find it generally absent); affiliativeness (does person prefer a socially isolated or affiliative life style, live in isolation, avoid joining an organization); social identification (does person come from a group perceived as pariah – minority, homosexual, motorcycle gang, teen-ager); primary group dissimulation (do family and friends protect, isolate, cover-up, creating greater or lesser visibility). These categories can be evaluated and contribute to an indice in the Associational Reaction Index.

Stigma – A rich literature exists on stigma, the process of spoiling an identity and the ways in which it is managed. Stigma can be defined as any flaw or defect with a negative effect on social acceptance. Goffman (1963: 108-109) states, "...the stigmatized individual defines himself as no different from any other human being, while at the same time he and those around him define him as someone apart."

One significant aspect of the labelling theory is related to the social reaction to deviance resulting in processes producing negative identities.

Two ideas central to these processes are "self-fulfilling prophecy" and "successful degradation ceremonies." W. I. Thomas (1927: 81) provided one of the basic principles in sociology: if people define situations as real, they are real in their consequences. This principle was elaborated by Merton (1957: 421-434) when he asserted that a definition of a situation may be false but the result in behavior may make the false conception come true. The primary deviant when publicly caught and labelled can become what we say he is. If treated like a criminal, he may act like one.

The successful degradation ceremony is an institutionalized means of stigmatizing an individual. As Garfinkel (1956: 420) argues, "...there is no society where social structure does not provide, in its routine features, the conditions of identity degradation." Garfinkel suggests that criminal proceedings are a kind of public branding – a status degradation ceremony. Goffman (1963) contends that the criminal justice system confers a spoiled identity through the process of arrest, adjudication, incarceration, and other aspects of the justice system. This process deprives a person of his reputation as worthy.

Identities may be spoiled, but the management of the spoiled identity (stigma management) is a normal process and can mitigate the consequences. The ability to manage a spoiled identity is significant in assessing the effect of stigma. Lemert (1976: 41) asserts, within the labelling framework, that secondary deviation is a common event while Goffman (1963) insists that the management of the spoiled identity makes secondary deviation rare. Sykes and Matza (1957) note that delinquents employ manifold rationalizing and projecting techniques to justify or neutralize the delinquent acts and maintain a sense of identity – "techniques of neutralization." Other mitigating devices include deviance desavowal, and "rejecting the rejectors." The social structure also contributes to ego and identity maintenance through ameliorating situations and ceremonies. The same system that may spoil an identity may also use means to prevent or restore the spoilage. The justice system includes pardons, executive clemency, and closed or destroyed records. Many deviants are protected from stigma or aided in managing it by family, church, and employers. Organizations try to normalize misbehavior and resist overt reaction, families frequently normalize misbehavior of members. Alcoholic Anonymous, narcotics anonymous, gamblers anonymous, and similar groups succeed often in relabeling a stigmatized deviant and restoring dignity.

The process of stigmatization is a complex one. There are different levels of stigma: consensual, or by an individual or group, or by an institution or association. Repetition of an activity can lead to stigma, to institutionalization, to permanacy. Once stigmatized, society may rationalize a label within a principle of infallibility in spite of any rehabilitative ideal – once a criminal, always a criminal. Stigma can occur without an act like Hellman's "Children's Hour" or the hysteria of child molestation and sexual psychopathy. On the other hand, eufunctional deviance is not stigmatized as it is managed by mechanisms like role suspension, rationalization, and rule suspension.

Some of the associational sources of stigma are a social expectation of failure, degradation ceremonies, and an outcast identity. Some of the sources of management are meliorating ceremonies and general institutional support. In measuring the contribution of stigma to associational reaction, the sources and management of stigma can be explored along three dimensions: does ego feel that his identity has been spoiled; what is the source of the spoilage; how well does ego manage the stigma?

The key to the effect of stigma lies with the spoiled rather than the spoiler. Thus the subject of analysis would be ego and not the structure. However, the source of stigmatization needs to be established so that the associational role in the process is evaluated. Finally, a spoiled identity is a common experience. At some time or other all egos are crushed. Yet most everyone manages it – except for some who have meagre resources to restore an identity. The effect of stigma can be measured by evaluating the felt stigma and the success in managing it. The resultant difference can be inserted into the calculations for the Index of Associational Reaction.

Social Tolerance – Social reaction involves visibility and stigma but in between is some magnitude of social tolerance. These three factors are linked when visibility leads to social intolerance which can lead to stigma which in turn can lead to intolerance. What is tolerated and what is opposed is dependent on several factors and is often capricious in time, place, and circumstances.

Social tolerance is the willingness on the part of various structural elements to do something about nonnormative behavior. This may range from simple rejection to the more serious intervention by enforcement agencies. Tolerance limits borders and encompasses a normative range of deviance beyond which lies disapproved or approved deviance. Though institutions essentially are interacting people, there are many instances where institutional intolerance of some behavior is tolerated by individuals in the institution. An institution may not tolerate drug use but many individuals in the institution may. Social tolerance should be distinguished from individual tolerance which is related to personality.

Intent has a significant influence on social tolerance. Is the act accidental, premeditated, reluctant, conspiratorial, a matter of normative ignorance (insanity or diminished capacity), involve an attractive nuisance, victim provoked, or episodic paranoia. The degree of the social reaction is directly related to the degree of intent.

The social reaction is tuned-in to perceived seriousness of the harm. External factors like the amount of injury, extent of a theft, target of the act, damage to property, or moral rectitude influence the kind and extent of a reaction. And in general, there is remarkable consensus as to the degree of seriousness of a crime (McCleary, et. al., 1981: 276).

The degree of social tolerance also is related to the status of the perpetrator and the victim. High status or high esteem actors have wider latitudes of nonconformity than actors of low status or low esteem (Hollander and Willis, 1967). The victim, too, is judged by status and esteem. The outrage is greater for the higher status victim. Social solidarity can impress a social reaction. Institutional tolerance is differentially distributed as an elite group or individual may be tolerated because of the perception of importance to group solidarity. In a study of social tolerance utilizing the social distance concept, there was toleration variation for several groups (Simmons 1969: 33). In order of increased intolerance, the groups were: intellectuals, ex-mental patients, atheists, ex-convicts, gamblers, alcoholics, prostitutes, and homosexuals.

There are structural differences in social tolerance – rural-urban, social class, ethnicity, gender, age, and others. Social tolerance is reflected in the assorted images attributed to the deviant (abetted by the media) from dangerous and evil to strange and heroic. Daniel Glaser (1971) notes that the tolerance of behavioral diversity varies directly with the division of labor. The more complex the society, the greater the tolerance of nonnormative behavior. Other effectors of social tolerance include the ideology of the community, conscience of the community, power elite, pressures for consensus, and the mass media. At times the reaction is ephemeral as the definition of the situation shifts. In a recent case a stowaway from South Africa landed in the United States. The media gave positive attention to his plight and he was offered sanctuary. Other similar illegal entries are managed less amiably. Social tolerance includes tacit concessions to deviant roles. In prostitution the role behavior is deviant but the allusive acceptance may obviate the person as deviant. Finally, tolerance does not lie in bed rock but changes as it navigates the tide of shifting passions.

There are many variables stimulating tolerance: intent, status of victim and deviant, harm, contribution to solidarity, several structural variables, community ideology, moral rectitude, and others. A measure of social tolerance should be possible employing the three variables of intent, harm, and status. There are many ways to measure social tolerance. Lemert (1951: 57-58) uses the idea of a "tolerance quotient," a ratio between actual criminal behavior and public attitudes toward that behavior. This constitutes an attempt to assess so-called crime waves. Jessor, et. al. (1968) devised a "tolerance of deviance measure." However, this was an evaluation of personality and not structure. Twelve deviant acts were listed and a person's acceptance or rejection of the acts were tallied. Perhaps such a technique could be adapted for associations.

Intent and social tolerance can be evaluated by specifying varying degrees of intent and varying degrees of social tolerance. This would assess a community's level of social tolerance as it is related to the intent involved in the deviant act. The intent can be specified in categories from premeditation to normative ignorance. The tolerance can be categorized in terms ranging from embracement to rejection. To explore further with more specificity, tolerance can be elaborated in terms of several associations, while intent can be elaborated in terms of several forms of deviance such as crimes vs. property, sex crimes, mental illness, and suicide. This can provide an index of associational tolerance based on intent.

Peoples' reaction to deviance is effected by the status of the victim and the deviant. In mental illness, the victim may be perceived as many individuals or an ambiguous public. In suicide the victim may be perceived as the deviant himself or others, like family members. At any rate, some measure of tolerance can be obtained by associating classes of status characteristics, for example, age, gender, occupation, social class, ethnicity, and degrees of tolerance. The tolerance can be specified in terms of different forms of deviance and specific cases of associations. The result would be an index of social tolerance as effected by status.

If an act is perceived as likely to harm others – many others – and diminish the solidarity of the community, it is less likely to be tolerated. If categories of harm (self-inflicted, family, workplace, and others) are related to categories of social reaction (ignored, mild rebuke, outrage, and others) some indication of the reaction to the perceived magnitude of harm can be calculated.

Combining the indices of intent, status, and harm results in an index of the level of social tolerance. Adding the Social Tolerance Index to that of stigma attribution and visibility results in an Associational Reaction Index. Finally, combining the Association Reaction Index with Association Bond Index, Association Coping Mechanism Index, results in an Index of Association Effectiveness.

Chapter V

Conclusion

As one reviews the history of deviance at least three things are clear. First, the level of abstraction and sophistication is considerably greater than it was. Second, each theory was liberally criticized and its limitations acknowledged. Third, too many of the theories received insufficient empirical support or suffered a shortage of empirical content. Demonology, lex taliones, hedonism, and the "born criminal" have survived in modified form, but have received scant empirical support, are limited in application, and are, more or less, dismissed. The two most popular approaches are the psychogenic and socio-cultural. The psychological approach focuses on personality and although neo-Freudianism and other offshoots have broadened the perspective, personality and its pathology still dominates. Too often functioning as a closed system rather than a theory, it still lacks substantial empirical support and remains clinically oriented. The socio-cultural approach emphasized environment and consists of a number of subdivisions. Historically, two have dominated the theoretical scene, Sutherland's "differential association," and Merton's "anomie." Both have had mixed empirical confirmation and are flawed by insufficient empirical content. The labelling approach seems to have peaked and like many others has escaped empirical verification. Yet, despite disparate evidence of success and failure, each has contributed something to the search for explanation. What could be useful is a synthesis of what is known presented in the form of a model, with a focus on empirical content for testing and verification, i.e. a deviance process linked to testable reality through operationalizing of the various constructs. Thus, personality becomes traits and coping mechanisms specified and measured by a personality inventory and an inventory to measure ways of mitigating stress, respectively.

A deviance model is proposed as $Df = (P \oplus C \oplus S)$ where D is deviance, P is personality, C is culture, S is structure, and $\oplus$ is more than simple addition. The elaboration of this model becomes $Df = [P (P_t, P_m) \oplus C (C_n, C_b, C_v, C_{cm}) \oplus S (S_r, S_s, S_a)]$.

P is personality and P_t and P_m are personality traits and personality coping mechanisms. P_t, P_m will adjust to produce different degrees of conforming personality summarized as conforming, ambivalent, and deviant personality. C is culture and C_n, C_b, C_v, C_{cm} are cultural norms, cultural beliefs, cultural values, and cultural coping mechanisms. C_n, C_b, C_v, C_{cm} will adjust to produce different degrees of conforming culture summarized as conforming, ambivalent, and deviant culture. S is structure and S_r, S_s, S_a are structural role, structural status, and structural association effectiveness. S_r, S_s, S_a will adjust to produce different degrees of conforming structure summarized as conforming, ambivalent, and deviant structure.

Each factor identified as determinants or the degree of conformity (e.g. P_t, C_{cm}, S_r) was indicated by establishing empirical content. P_t is derived through an assessment of self-esteem, sensitivity to social influence, capacity for change, impulsivity, empathy, hostility, responsibility, intellectual efficiency, socialization, anxiety level, dominance, self-discipline, and masculinity-femininity. P_m is derived through an assessment of fantasy, suppression, rationalization, projection, withdrawal, denial, reaction-formation, optimism and fatalism, across situations involving home, occupation, peers, and authority. Combining the results of P_t and P_m provides and Index of Congeniality with conformity summarized as conforming personality, ambivalent personality, deviant personality.

The same approach established similar summaries of conformity for culture and structure. The four attributes of culture (C_b, C_v, C_n, C_{cm}) were explored for empirical content. C_b is divided into three categories: philosophical/religious, economic/political, scientific/technological. Subjects can be assessed for the dominant category and compared to society's dominant belief system. C_v evaluation can utilize the work of Rokeach (1973; 1979) which measures 18 "terminal values" and 18 "instrumental values." A comparison of a subject's values with an established reference controlled for demographics will produce a score to contribute to the measure of culture's contribution to conformity/deviance. C_n measures the complex normative system's contribution to conformity/deviance. Norms are classified as technical, secondary, primary, moral, and fanatical. Each type norm is related to three levels of sentiment: pre-proscriptive, preferential, and permissive. The norm types with their implied amount of sentiment are explored in three dimensions to determine an index or profile for inclusion in the cultural contribution to conformity/deviance. The three dimensions are situational (family, friends, institutions), real-ideal behavior, and status/role (plebian, centurian, imperator). C_{cm} is classified into four categories: cathartic, collective, egoistic, and transitory. Each category is assessed across self, family, peers, and institutions. Within this paradigm an appropriate device would approximate the magnitude of the ability to guard against the strain toward deviance.

The salient features of structure for deviance are role, status, and associations – S_r, S_s, S_a respectively. S_r is measured by the number of roles played, the amount of role conflict, and skill in role-taking. These variables are evaluated among salient social institutions resulting in an Index of Role Sufficiency.

S_s is appraised through a capacity for status, status consistency, status adaptation, and status occupancy. This results in an Index of Status Stability. S_a explores three specific aspects of associations: associational bonds, coping mechanisms, and reaction (visibility, tolerance, and stigma). The evaluation of these three aspects of associations' relationship to conformity/deviance leads to an Index of Association Effectiveness.

In summary, the mathematical model of deviance is a functional one where deviance is a function of personality, culture, and structure. Personality is the combined indices of traits and coping mechanisms into an Index of Personality. Culture is the combined indices of beliefs, norms, values, coping mechanisms forming an Index of Culture. Structure is the combined indices of role, status, and associations forming an Index of

96

Structure. The variables can be quantified in a standardized form and when appropriate, weighted and then combined into indexes. The combined indexes assess the contributions to conformity/deviance summarized as conformity-ambivalence-deviance.

Figure 5.1

NEGOTIATING SOCIAL GAUNTLET TOWARD CONFORMITY OR DEVIANCE

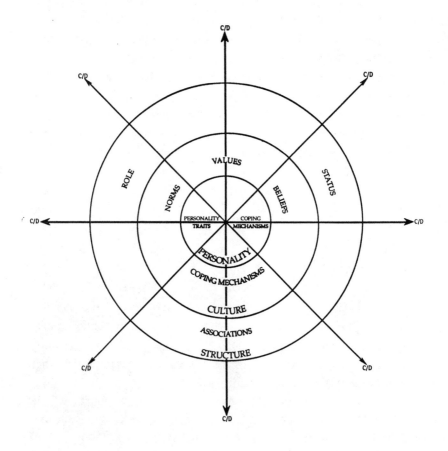

FIGURE 5.2

PERSONALITY ⊕ CULTURE ⊕ STRUCTURE AND DEVIANCE

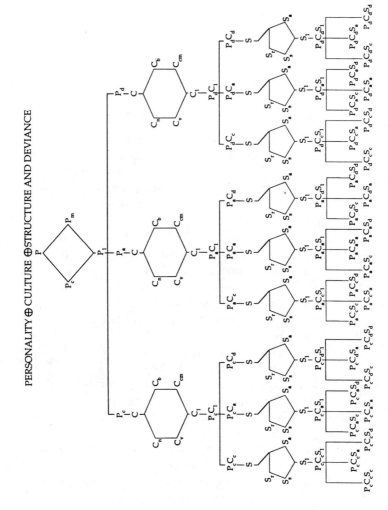

98

Legend:

P : Personality
P_t : Personality traits
P_m : Personality coping mechanisms
P_1 : Personality Index of Conformity
P_c : Conforming personality
P_a : Ambivalent personality
P_d : Deviant personality
C : Culture
C_n : Cultural norms
C_b : Cultural beliefs
C_v : Cultural values
C_{cm} : Cultural coping mechanisms
C_1 : Cultural Index of Conformity
P_cC_1 : Conforming personality, cultural index
P_cC_c : Conforming personality, conforming culture
P_cC_a : Conforming personality, ambivalent culture
P_cC_d : Conforming personality, deviant culture
P_aC_c : Ambivalent personality, conforming culture
P_aC_a : Ambivalent personality, ambivalent culture
P_aC_d : Ambivalent personality, deviant culture
P_dC_c : Deviant personality, conforming culture
P_dC_a : Deviant personality, ambivalent culture
P_dC_d : Deviant personality, deviant culture
S : Structure
S_r : Structural role sufficiency
S_s : Structural status stability
S_a : Structural associational effectiveness
S_1 : Structural Index of Conformity
$P_cC_cS_1$: Conforming personality, conforming culture, structural index
$P_cC_cS_c$: Conforming personality, conforming culture conforming structure
$P_cC_cS_a$: Conforming personality, conforming culture ambivalent structure
$P_cC_cS_d$: Conforming personality, conforming culture deviant structure

$P_cC_aS_c$: Conforming personality, ambivalent culture
conforming structure

$P_cC_aS_a$: Conforming personality, ambivalent culture
ambivalent structure

$P_cC_aS_d$: Conforming personality, ambivalent culture
deviant structure

$P_cC_dS_c$: Conforming personality, deviant culture
conforming structure

$P_cC_dS_a$: Conforming personality, deviant culture
ambivalent structure

$P_cC_dS_d$: Conforming personality, deviant culture
deviant structure

$P_aC_cS_c$: Ambivalent personality, conforming culture
conforming structure

$P_aC_cS_a$: Ambivalent personality, conforming culture
ambivalent structure

$P_aC_cS_d$: Ambivalent personality, conforming culture
deviant structure

$P_aC_aS_c$: Ambivalent personality, ambivalent culture
conforming structure

$P_aC_aS_a$: Ambivalent personality, ambivalent culture
ambivalent structure

$P_aC_aS_d$: Ambivalent personality, ambivalent culture
deviant structure

$P_aC_dS_c$: Ambivalent personality, deviant culture
conforming structure

$P_aC_dS_a$: Ambivalent personality, deviant culture
ambivalent structure

$P_aC_dS_d$: Ambivalent personality, deviant culture
deviant structure

$P_dC_cS_c$: Deviant personality, conforming culture
conforming structure

$P_dC_cS_a$: Deviant personality, conforming culture
ambivalent structure

$P_dC_cS_d$: Deviant personality, conforming culture
deviant structure

RASMUSON LIBRARY
UNIVERSITY OF ALASKA-FAIRBANKS

$P_dC_aS_c$: Deviant personality, ambivalent culture
conforming structure

$P_dC_aS_a$: Deviant personality, ambivalent culture
ambivalent structure

$P_dC_aS_d$: Deviant personality, ambivalent culture
deviant structure

$P_dC_dS_c$: Deviant personality, deviant culture
conforming structure

$P_dC_dS_a$: Deviant personality, deviant culture
ambivalent structure

$P_dC_dS_d$: Deviant personality, deviant culture
deviant structure

The general proposition is that the more conforming the personality, culture, and structure, the greater the probability for conformity; the more deviant the personality, culture, and structure, the greater the probability for deviance.

Deviance is a social and not an individual phenomenon. The context for such variables as visibility, tolerance, solidarity, goes beyond the group within which the act occurs. In modern society deviance is defined within a larger context of a community, county, state, nation, and at times, the world. The same process accounts for change from deviant to non-deviant, often referred to as rehabilitation. Why a person chooses one course of action over another is a major premise for deviance theory permitting explanation as well as mapping the complex process. Homans (1967) offers a psychological premise – the higher the value, as perceived by the actor, of a reward, the more likely the action will occur in a direction toward that reward. However, this assumption is not always true in deviance, unless the explanation becomes tautological. The thief may steal to embarrass his parents; the sexual assault may be an attack upon his mother. One might say in each case satisfaction was the reward of higher value than the morality of conformity. But then the deviant act begs the question – as any deviant act must be interpreted as possessing higher value.

The broader model includes the personality dimension, but extends it to the influences of the environment through an ongoing socialization process. This links all aspects of the complex process of deviancy and forgoes a deterministic for a stochastic explanation. Deviance is a dynamic, relative, interaction process.

The model implicitly or explicitly incorporates several extant theories of deviance. The psychogenic explanations are observed in the evaluation of personality traits (P_t) and coping mechanisms (P_{cm}). Labelling is approached through the inclusion in the structural dimension with stigma and audience reaction (S_a). Anomie theory appears in the cultural context with values (C_v), beliefs (C_b), and norms (C_n). Differential association receives attention in several places, association (S_a), culture (C_n,C_{cm}), structure (S_r). Ecological studies appear in such indices as $C_n,C_v,C_b,C_{cm},S_r,S_s,S_a$. Other theories include cultural conflict (cultural index), subcultural theories (culture and structure indices, and personality coping mechanisms), and containment theory is strongly represented in all categories (personality, culture, structure). Even the biogenic approach is implicitly included (admittedly in a very limited and indirect way) by use of personality traits that bear some reflection of ego's reaction to biological phenomena.

Some theorists postulate positive and negative deviance. Some deviance can be creative rather than destructive. This notion is reflected in the tolerance index (S_a). If a person is deviant in personality and culture, he is less apt to be creative; if the deviance is low in probability and only in certain aspects of personality, culture, and/or structure, he is more apt to be creative. The model limits what is deviant to consensual beliefs that the act(s) threaten to reduce solidarity.

Particular attention was paid to establishing an empirical route to testing, illustrating the empirical content of the model. Testing should lead to adjustments to the various indices without effecting the principles. For example, ex-post-facto studies can test the contribution of personality traits or other variables. The addition or subtraction or modification of these variables would fine tune the assessments. Subcultures and different structural environments can be portrayed and their specific contributions to conformity/deviance established. Comparative studies of deviance would be possible. Approaching deviance in this manner can enhance explanation and establish predictions leading to education and reforms that influence and clarify the conformity/deviance enigma. Explaining deviance in this processional manner, which also summarizes existing knowledge and offers opportunity for testing and verification, can insert sufficiency in the quest for explanation.

REFERENCES

Abrahamsen, David, 1952. *Who Are the Guilty? A Study of Education and Crime*. New York: Holt, Rinehart and Winston.

Adams, Stuart. 1953. "Status Congruency as a Variable in Small Group Performance." *Social Forces*, 32: 16-22.

Aichorn, August. 1953. *Wayward Youth*. New York: The Viking Press, Inc.

Allport, Gordon W. 1937. *Personality: A Psychological Interpretation*. New York: Holt.

Bateson, Gregory. 1942a. "Some Systematic Approaches to the Study of Culture and Personality." *Character and Personality*, 11: 76-84.

_____. 1944. "Cultural Determinants of Personality." In J. McV. Hunt, (Ed.), *Personality and the Behavior Disorders*, Volume 2: 714-735 New York: Ronald.

_____. 1958. *Naven*. Second Edition. Stanford: Stanford University Press.

_____. 1942b. "Morale and National Character." In G. Watson, (Ed.), *Civilian Morale*. Boston: Society For the Psychological Study of Social Issues, 74-89.

Beccaria, Cesare. 1819. *An Essay On Crime and Punishment*. Philadelphia: Phillip H. Nicklin.

Becker, Howard S. 1950. *Through Values To Social Interpretation*. Durham, North Carolina: University of North Carolina.

_____. 1963. *Outsiders*. New York: The Free Press.

Bell Wendell. 1957. "Anomie, Social Isolation, and the Class Structure." *Sociometry*, 20: 105-116.

Bendix, Reinhard. 1960. *Max Weber An Intellectual Portrait*. New York: Doubleday and Company, Inc.

_____. and Seymour M. Lipset. 1966. *Class, Status and Power*. Second Edition. New York: The Free press.

Benedict, Ruth F. 1934. *Patterns of Culture*. Boston: Houghton Mifflin.

_____. 1938. "Continuities and Discontinuities in Cultural Conditioning." *Psychiatry*, 1: 161-167.

_____. 1946a. *The Chrysanthemum and the Sword*. Boston: Houghton Mifflin.

104

_____. 1946b. *The Study of Cultural Patterns in European Nations.* Trans. New York Academy of Science 8 (Series II): 274-279.

Berger, Peter. 1963. *Invitation to Sociology: A Humanistic Perspective.* New York: Anchor.

_____and Thomas Luckmann. 1966. *The Social Construction of Reality.* New York: Doubleday.

_____, Joseph M. Hamit Fisek, Robert Z. Norman, and Morris Zelditch Jr. 1977. *Status Characteristics and Social Interaction.* New York: Elsvier.

Bergsma, Lily Chu. 1977. *Cross-Cultural Study of Conformity in American and Chinese.* San Francisco: R & E Research Associates.

Biddle, Bruce J. and Edwin J. Thomas (Eds.). 1966. *Role Theory: Concepts and Research.* New York: Wiley

Bierstedt, Robert. 1974. *The Social Order.* Fourth Edition. New York: McGraw-Hill Book Company.

Birenbaum, Arnold and Edward Sagarin. 1964. *Norms, Values, and Human Behavior.* New York: Praeger Publishers.

Blake, Judith and Kingsley Davis. 1964. "Norms, Values, and Sanctions." In *Handbook of Modern Sociology.* Edited by Robert E. L. Faris. Chicago: Rand McNally, 456-466.

Blau, Peter M. (Ed.). 1975. *Approaches to the Study of Social Structure.* New York: The Free Press.

Blumer, Herbert. 1969. *Symbolic Interactionism: Perspective and Method.* New York: Prentice-Hall, Inc.

Boas, Frank. 1911. *The Mind of Primitive Man.* New York: Macmillan.

Boskoff, Alvin. 1972. *The Mosaic of Sociological Theory.* New York: Thomas Y. Crowell Co.

Bosserman, P. 1977. "Changing Core Values in American Society." Presented at the 72d Annual Meeting of the American Sociological Society, New York.

Cameron, Norman. 1960. "Role Concepts in Behavior Pathology." *American Journal of Sociology*, 55: 464-467.

Carroll, John B. (Ed.). 1956. *Language, Thought and Reality. Selected Writings of Benjamin Lee Whorf.* Boston: Technology Press of Massachusetts Institute of Technology.

Catton, William R. Jr. 1959. "A Theory of Value." *American Sociological Review*, 24: 310-317.

Cloward, Richard A. and Lloyd E. Ohlin. 1960. *Delinquency and Opportunity: A Theory of Delinquent Gangs.* New York: The Free Press of Glencoe.

Cohen, Albert K. 1966. *Deviance and Control.* Englewood Cliffs, New Jersey: Prentice-Hall, Inc.

Cohen, Stanley and Andrew Scull (Eds.). 1983. *Social Control and the State.* New York: St. Martin's Press.

Coleman, L. 1944. "What Is American?" *Social Forces*, 19: 492-499.

Cooley, Charles H. 1922. *Human Nature and the Social Order.* New York: Charles Scribner's Sons.

Cleckley, Harvey. 1964. *The Mask of Sanity.* Fourth Edition. St. Louis: Mosby Co.

Cohen, Albert K. 1955. *Delinquent Boys: The Culture of the Gang.* New York: The Free Press.

Dahrendorf, Ralf. 1970. "On the Origin of Inequality Among Men." In Edward O. Laumann, Paul M. Siegel, and Robert W. Hodge, (Eds.), *The Logic of Social Hierarchies.* Chicago: Markham Publishing Co., 3-30.

Dai, Bingham. 1948. "Some Problems of Personality Development Among Negro Children." In Clyde Kluckhohn and Henry A. Murray, (Eds.), *Personality in Nature, Society, and Culture.* New York: Knopf, 437-458.

Davis, Kingsly. 1942. "A Conceptual Analysis of Stratification." *American Sociological Review*, 7: 309-321.

_____ and Wilbert E. Moore. 1945. "Some Principles of Stratification". *American Sociological Review*, 10: 242- 249.

_____ 1949. *Human Society.* New York: Macmillan Co.

De Tocqueville, Alexis. 1945. *Democracy in America.* Volume I, New York: Vintage.

Devereux, George. 1951. *Reality and Dream.* New York: International University Press.

DeVos, George. 1961. "Symbolic Analysis in the Cross- Cultural Study of Personality." In Bert Kaplan, (Ed.), *Studying Personality Cross-Culturally.* New York: Harper & Row, 599-634.

_____ 1964. "Role Narcissism and the Etiology of Japanese Suicide." Paper read at First International Congress of Social Psychiatry. London: August.

_____ and Arthur A. Hippler. 1969. "Cultural Psychology: Comparative Studies in Human Behavior." In Gardner Lindzey and Elliot Aronson, (Eds.), *Handbook of Social Psychology*. Second Edition. Reading, Mass.: Addison-Wesley Publishing Co., Vol. 4, 323-417.

Douglas, Jack D. 1970. "Deviance and Respectability: The Social Construction of Moral Meaning." In Jack D. Douglas, (Ed.), *Deviance and Respectability*. New York: Basic Books, Inc., 3-30.

Dubin, Robert. 1969. *Theory Building*. New York: The Free Press.

DuBois, Cora. 1944. *The People of Alor*. Minneapolis: University of Minnesota Press.

_____ 1955. "The Dominant Value Profile of American Culture." *American Anthropology*, 57: 1232-1239.

Durkheim, Emile. 1951. *Suicide: A Study in Sociology*. Translated by John A. Spaulding and George Simpson. George Simpson (Ed.), New York: The Free Press.

_____. 1954. *The Elementary Forms of the Religious Life*. Translated by Joseph Ward Swain. Glencoe, Illinois: The Free Press. Originally Published in 1912.

_____. 1964. *The Division of Labor in Society*. Translated by George Simpson. New York: The Free Press. Originally Published in 1893.

Edgerton, Robert B. 1967. *The Cloak of Competence*. Berkeley: University of California Press.

Erickson, Bonnie and H. and T. A. Nosanchuk. 1984. "The Allocation of Esteem and Disesteem: A Test of Goode's Theory." *American Sociological Review*, 49: 648-658.

Erikson, Kai T. 1957. "Patient Role and Social Uncertainty." *Psychiatry: Journal for the Study of Interpersonal Processes*, 20, (August).

_____. 1962. "Notes on the Sociology of Deviance." *Social Problems*, 9: 308.

Erikson, Maynard L. and La Mar T. Empey. 1963. "Court Records, Undetected Delinquency and Decision-Making." *Journal of Criminal Law, Criminology & Police Science*, 54: 456-469.

Faris, Robert E. L. 1955. *Social Disorganization*. New York: Ronald Press Co.

Fink, Arthur E. 1938. *Causes of Crime: Biological Theories in the United States, 1800-1915*. Philadelphia: University of Pennsylvania Press.

Frazier, Sir James George. 1970. *The Golden Bough*. New York: George Macy Companies, Inc. Originally Published in 1890, expanded versions followed in 1900 and 1911-1915.

Freud, Sigmund. 1949. *An Outline of Psychoanalysis*. New York: Morton.

_____.1952. *General Introduction to Psychoanalysis*. Revised edition translated by Joan Rivieri. New York: Garden City Books.

Fromm, Erich. 1941. *Escape From Freedom*. New York: Farrar & Rinehart.

_____. 1963. *Childhood and Society*. Second Edition. New York: W.W. Norton and Co., Inc.

Finestone, Harold. 1957. "Cats, Kicks, and Color." *Social Problems*, 5: 3-13.

Garfinkel, Harold. 1956. "Conditions of Successful Degradation Ceremonies." *American Journal of Sociology*, 61: 420-424.

_____. 1964. "Studies of the Routine Grounds of Everyday Activities." *Social Problems*, 11: 225-250.

Geschwender, James A. 1970. "Continuities in Theories of Status Consistency and Cognitive Dissonance." In Edward O. Laumann, Paul M. Siegel, Robert W. Hodge, (Eds.), *The Logic of Social Hierarchies*. Chicago: Markham Publishing Co., 500-511.

Gibbs, Jack P. and Walter T. Martin. 1958. "A Theory of Status Integration and Its Relationship to Suicide." *American Sociological Review*, 23: 140-147.

_____. 1964. *Status Integration and Suicide*. Oregon: University of Oregon Books.

_____. 1981. *Norms, Deviance, and Social Control*. New York: Elsevier North Holland, Inc.

Giddings, Franklin H. 1907. *The Elements of Sociology*. New York: Macmillan.

Gillin, J. 1955. "National and Regional Cultural Values in the United States." *Social Forces*, 34: 107-113.

Glabb, E.G. 1981. "The Ranking of Self-Actualization Values." *Sociological Quarterly*, 22: 373-383.

108

Glaser, Daniel. 1971. "Criminology and Public Policy." *The American Sociologist*, 6: 32.

_____. 1978. *Crime In Our Changing Society*. New York: Holt, Rinehart & Winston.

Glasser, William. 1965. *Reality Therapy*: A New Approach to Psychiatry. New York: Harper & Row.

Goffman, Erving. 1959a. "The Moral Character of the Mental Patient." *Psychiatry*, 22: 123-142.

_____. 1959b. *The Presentation of the Self in Everyday Life*. Garden City, New York: Doubleday.

_____. 1961. *Encounters: Two Studies in the Sociology of Interaction*. Indianapolis, Indiana: Bobbs-Merrill.

_____. 1963. *Stigma, Notes on the Management of Spoiled Identity*. Englewood Cliffs, New Jersey: Prentice-Hall, Inc.

_____. 1967. *Interaction Ritual*. Garden City, New York: Anchor Books.

_____. 1983. "The Interaction Order." *American Sociological Review*, 48: 1-17.

Goode, William J. 1960. "A Theory of Role Strain." *American Sociological Review*, 25: 483-496.

Gorer, Geoffrey. 1943. *Themes in Japanese Culture*. New York Academy of Science, 5 (Series II): 106-124.

_____. 1948. *The American People*. New York: Norton.

Gough, Harrison. 1947. "A Sociological Theory of Psychopathy." *American Journal of Sociology*, 53: 359-366.

Gouldner, Alvin W. 1976. *The Dialectic of Ideology and Technology*. New York: Seabury.

Gross, Edward and Gregory P. Stone. 1965. "Embarrassment and the Analysis of Role Requirements." *American Journal of Sociology*, 70: 1-15.

Gullahorn, John T. 1956. "Measuring Role Conflict." *American Journal of Sociology*, 61: 299-303.

Gusfield, Joseph R. 1975. "Status Conflicts and the Changing Ideologies of the American Temperance Movement." In F. James Davis and Richard Stivers, (Eds.), *The Collective Definition of Deviance*. New York: The Free Press, 222- 240.

Hall, Calvin S. and Gardner Lindzey. 1957. *Theories of Personality.* New York: John Wiley & Sons, Inc.

Hallowell, A. Irving. 1960. "Ojibwa Ontology, Behavior, and World View." In Stanley Diamond, (Eds.), *Culture in History, Essays in Honor of Paul A. Radin.* New York: Columbia University Press.

Hawkins, Richard and Gary Tiedman. 1975. *The Creation of Deviance.* Columbus Ohio: Charles E. Merril Publishing Co.

Healy, William and Augusta Bronner. 1936. *New Light on Delinquency and Its Treatment.* New Haven, Connecticut: Yale University.

Heussenstamm, F. K. 1971. "Bumper Stickers and the Cops." *Transaction,* 8: 32-33.

Hirschi, Travis. 1969. *Causes of Delinquency.* Berkeley: University of California Press.

Hofstede, Gort. 1980. *Culture's Consequences.* Beverly Hills: Sage Publications.

Hollander, Edwin P. and Richard H. Willis. 1967. "Some Current Issues in the Psychology of Conformity and Nonconformity." *Psychological Bulletin,* 68: 62-76.

Homans, George C. 1961. *Social Behavior.* New York: Harcourt, Brace and World.

_____. 1967. *The Nature of Social Science.* New York: Harcourt, Brace and World.

Honigmann, John J. 1949. *Culture and Ethos of Kaska Society.* Yale University Publications in Anthropology. No. 40. New Haven: Yale University Press.

Hooton, Ernest A. 1939. *Crime and the Man.* Cambridge, Mass.: Harvard University Press.

Hornung, Carlton A. 1977. "Social Status, Status Consistency and Psychological Stress." *American Sociological Review,* 42: 623-638.

Hyman, Herbert. 1953. "The Value Systems of Different Classes." In Reinhard Bendix and Seymour M. Lipset, (Eds.), *Class, Status, and Power.* Second Edition. New York: Free Press.

Inciardi, James A. 1978. *Reflections on Crime.* New York: Holt, Rinehart & Winston.

Inkeles, Alex. 1959. "Personality and Social Structure." In Robert K. Merton, et. al., (Eds), *Sociology Today*. New York: Basic Books, 249-276.

_____. 1961. "National Character and Modern Political Systems." In Francis L. K. Hsu, (Ed.), *Psychological Anthropology: Approaches to Culture and Personality*. Homewood, Illinois: Wiley.

_____. 1966. "The Modernization of Man." In M. Weiner, (Ed.), *Modernization*. New York: Basic Books, 138-151.

_____. and Daniel J. Levinson. 1969. "National Character: The Study of Modal Personality and Sociocultural Systems." In Gardner Lindzey and Elliot Aronson, (Eds.), *The Handbook of Social Psychology*. Second Edition, Volume. 4. Reading, Mass.: Addison-Wesley Publishing Co., 418-506.

_____. 1977. "Continuity and Change in the American National Character." Presented at the 72d Annual Meeting of the American Sociological Association, New York.

Jackson, Elton F. 1962. "Status Consistency and Symptoms of Stress." *American Sociological Review*, 27: 469-480.

Jaeger, Gertrude and Philip Selznick. 1964. "A Normative Theory of Culture." *American Sociological Review* 29: 653-669.

Jessor, Richard, et. al. 1968. *Society, Personality, and Deviant Behavior*. New York: Holt, Rinehart & Winston.

Kahl, Joseph A. 1965. "Some Measures of Achievement Orientation." *American Journal of Sociology*, 70: 669- 681.

Kaplan, Howard B. 1975. "Sequelae of Self-Derogation: Predicting From a General Theory of Deviant Behavior." *Youth and Society*, 7: 171-197.

Kardiner, Abram. 1939. *The Individual and His Society*. New York: Columbia University Press.

_____. 1945a. "The Concept of Basic Personality Structure As An Operational Tool in the Social Sciences." In Ralph Linton, (Ed.), *The Science of Man in the World Crises*. New York: Columbia University Press, 107-122.

_____. with the collaboration of Robert Linton, Cora DuBois, and J. West. 1945b. *The Psychological Frontiers of Society*. New York: Columbia University Press.

Kemper, Theodore D. 1966. "Representative Roles and the Legitimation of Deviance." *Social Problems*, 13: 288-298.

Kephart, William M. 1954. "Negro Visibility." *American Sociological Review*, 19: 462-467.

Kessler, Ronald C. and Marilyn Essex. 1982. "Marital Status and Depression: The Importance of Coping Resources." *Social Forces*, 61: 484-507.

Kitsuse, John I. 1964. "Societal Reaction to Deviant Behavior: Problems of Theory and Method." In Howard S. Becker, (Ed.), *The Other Side*. New York: The Free Press, 87-102.

Klapp, Orrin E. 1973. *Models of Social Order*. Palo Alto, California: National Press.

Kluckhohn, Clyde. 1944. *Navaho Witchcraft*. Cambridge, Mass.: Peabody Museum of American Archeology and Ethnology.

_____. 1951. "Values and Value Orientation in the Theory of Action." In Talcott Parsons and Edward A. Shils, (Eds.), *Toward a General Theory of Action*. New York: Harper.

_____. 1961. "The Study of Values." In D. N. Barrett, (Ed.), *Values in America*. South Bend, Indiana: University of Notre Dame Press.

Kluckhohn, Florence. 1950. "Dominant and Substitute Profiles of Cultural Orientations." *Social Forces*, 28: 376-393.

_____. and Fred L. Strodtbeck. 1961. *Variations in Value Orientations*. Bloomington, Indiana: Row, Peterson.

Kohn, Melvin L. and Carmi Schooler. 1969. "Class, Occupation, and Orientation." *American Sociological Review*, 34: 626-633.

_____. 1977. *Class and Conformity*. Chicago: University of Chicago Press.

Kretschmer, Ernst. 1925. *Physique and Character*. Translated by W.J.H. Sprott. London: Kegan Paul, Trench, Trubner.

Kroeber, A. L. and Talcott Parsons. 1958. "The Concepts of Culture and Social System." *American Sociological Review*, 23: 582-583.

_____. and Clyde Kluckhohn. 1963. Culture, *A Critical Review of Concepts and Definitions*. New York: Vintage Books.

LaBarre, Weston. 1946. "Some Observations on Character Structure in the Orient: The Japanese." *Psychiatry*, 8: 319-342.

LaPiere, Richard T. 1954. *A Theory of Social Control*. New York: McGraw-Hill.

Lavater, John Caspar. 1775. *Physiognomical Fragments*. Zurich.

Lefley, Harriet P. 1972. "Modal Personality in the Bahamas." Journal of Cross-Cultural Psychology, 3: 135-147.

Leighton, Alexander H. 1945. The Governing of Men. Princeton: Princeton University Press.

Lemert, Edwin M. 1951. Social Pathology: A Systematic Approach to the Theory of Sociopathic Behavior. New York: McGraw-Hill.

_____. 1967. Human Deviance, Social Problems and Social Control. Englewood Cliffs, New Jersey: Prentice-Hall, Inc.

_____. 1974. "Beyond Mead: The Societal Reaction to Deviance." Social Problems, 21: 457-468.

_____. 1979, "Role Enactment, Self, and Identity in the Systematic Check Forger." In Delos H. Kelly, Deviant Behavior. New York: St. Martin's Press.

Lenski, Gerhard E. 1954. "Status Crystallization: A Non-Vertical Dimension of Social Status." American Sociological Review. 19: 405-413.

_____. 1956. "Social Participation and Status Crystallization." American Sociological Review. 21: 458- 464.

_____. 1966. Power and Privilege. New York: McGraw-Hill.

Levinson, Daniel J. 1961. "Role Personality and Social Structure in the Organizational Setting." In Seymour Martin Lipset and Neil J. Smelser, (Eds.), Sociology: The Progress of a Decade. Englewood Cliffs, New Jersey: Prentice-Hall, Inc., 299-311.

Lin, T.Y. 1958. "Tai-Pan and Liu-man: Two Types of Delinquent Youth in Chinese Society." British Journal of Delinquency, 8: 244-256.

Lindzey, Gardner and Elliot Aronson (Eds.), 1969. The Handbook of Social Psychology. Second Edition. Volume 4. Reading, Mass.: Addison-Wesley Publishing Co.

Linton, Ralph. 1936. The Study of Man. New York: D. Appleton Century Co.

_____. 1945. The Cultural Background of Personality. New York: Appleton-Century-Crofts.

_____. 1949. "Problems of Status Personality." In S.S. Sargent and Marion W. Smith, (Eds.), Culture and Personality. New York: Viking Fund, 163-173.

Lipset, Seymour M. 1963. *The First New Nation*. Garden City, New York: Anchor.

Liska, Allen E. and Mark D. Reed. 1985. "Ties to Conventional Institutions and Delinquency: Estimating Reciprocal Effects." *American Sociological Review*, 50: 547-560.

Lowie, Robert H. 1948. *Social Organization*. New York: Rinehart and Co.

Lombroso, Cesare. 1918. *Crime: Its Causes and Remedies*. Boston: Little, Brown and Co.

Malinowski, Bronislaw. 1948. *Magic, Science and Religion*. Glencoe Illinois: The Free Press.

_____. 1959. *Crime and Custom in Savage Society*. Paterson, New Jersey: Littlefield, Adams and Co.

Mandel, Michael J. 1983. "Local Roles and Social Networks." *American Sociological Review*, 48: 376-386.

Mannheim, Karl. 1957. *Systematic Sociology*. New York: Grove Press, Inc., 131-135.

Marwell, Gerald and Jerald Hage. 1970. "The Organization of Role-Relationships: A Systematic Description." *American Sociological Review*, 35: 884-900.

McCall, George J. 1963. "Symbiosis: The Case of Hoodoo and the Numbers Racket." *Social Problems*, 10: 361-371.

McCleary, Richard, Michael J. O'Neil, Thomas Epperlein, Constance Jones, Ronald H. Gray. 1981. "Effects of Legal Education and Work Experience on Perceptions of Crime Seriousness." *Social Problems*, 28: 277-289.

Mead, George H. 1934. *Mind, Self and Society*. Chicago: University of Chicago Press.

Mead, Margaret. 1942. *And Keep Your Powder Dry: An Anthropologist Looks at America*. New York: Morrow.

_____. 1951. *Soviet Attitudes Toward Authority*. New York: McGraw-Hill.

Merton, Robert K. 1957a. *Social Theory and Social Structure*. Glencoe: Illinois: The Free Press, chapters XII and XIII.

_____. 1957b. *Social Theory and Social Structure*. Revised Edition. New York: Free Press, 131-194.

_____. 1967. On *Theoretical Sociology*. New York: The Free Press.

114

Miller, Walter B. 1958. "Lower Class as a Generating Milieu of Gang Delinquency." *Journal of Social Issues*, 14: 5-19.

Mills, C. Wright. 1943. "The Professional Ideology of Social Pathologists." *American Journal of Sociology*, 49: 165- 180.

_____. 1951. White Collar: *The American Middle Class*. New York: Oxford University Press.

_____. 1956. *The Power Elite*. New York: Oxford University Press.

Miner, Horace and George DeVos. 1960. "Oasis and Casbah: Algerian Culture and Personality in Change." *Anthropology Papers*. University of Michigan. No. 15.

Mizushima, K. and George DeVos. 1962. *Research on Delinquency in Japan: An Introductory Review*. Unpublished manuscript.

Montagu, Ashley. 1967. *The American Way of Life*. New York: G.P. Putnam's Sons.

Morris, Charles. 1942. *Paths of Life*. New York: Harper.

_____. 1956. *Varieties of Human Value*. Chicago: University of Chicago.

_____. 1964. *Signification and Significance*. Cambridge: MIT Press.

Mukerjee, R. 1946. "The Sociology of Values." *Journal of Sociology and Social Research*, 31: 101-109.

Murphy, H. B. M. 1959. "Culture and Mental Disorder in Singapore." In M. K. Opler (Ed.), *Culture and Mental Health*. New York: Macmillan, 291-318.

Myrdal, Gunnar. 1944. *An American Dilemma*. New York: Harper.

Meyers, John W. and Phillip E. Hammond. 1971. "Forms of Status Inconsistency." *Social Forces*, 50: 91-101.

Nadel. S. F. 1957. *The Theory of Social Structure*. Glencoe, Illinois: The Free Press.

Nash, Jeffrey E. 1981. "Relations in Frozen Places: Observations on Winter Public Order." *Qualitative Sociology*, 4: 229-243.

Neiman, Lionel J. And James W. Hughes. 1951. "The Problem of the Concept of Role: A Resurvey of the Literature." *Social Forces*, 30: 141-149.

Newcomb, Theodore M. 1950. *Social Psychology*. New York: Dryden-Holt.

Nisbet, Robert A. 1970. *The Social Bond.* New York: Alfred A. Knopf.

Opler, Morris E. 1945. "Themes as Dynamic Forces in Culture." *American Journal of Sociology*, 51: 198-206.

Ossowski, Stanislaw. 1963. *Class Structure in the Social Consciousness.* London: Routledge & Kegan Paul.

Pareto, Vilfredo. 1935. *The Mind and Society.* Edited by Arthur Livingston, four volumes. New York: Arcourt, Brace and Co. This is a translation of the Ponderous Trattato di Sociologia Generale.

Parsons, Talcott. 1939. *The Structure of Social Action.* New York: Free Press.

_____. and Edward A. Shills, (Eds.). 1951a. *Toward A General Theory of Action.* New York: Harper & Row Publishers.

_____. 1951b. *The Social System.* Glencoe, Illinois: The Free Press of Glencoe.

_____. Edward A. Shils, and Robert F. Bales. 1953. *Working Papers in the Theory of Action.* New York: Free Press.

_____. 1954. *Essays in Sociological Theory.* Revised Edition. Glencoe, Illinois: The Free Press.

_____. and James Olds. 1955. "Mechanisms of Personality Functioning with Special Reference to Socialization." In Talcott Parsons and Robert F. Bales. *Family, Socialization and Interaction Process.* Glencoe, Illinois: The Free Press.

_____. 1961. "An Outline of the Social System." In Talcott Parsons, Edward A. Shils, Kaspar D. Naegele, and Jesse R. Pitts, (Eds.), *Theories of Society*, 30-79.

_____. 1966. *Societies.* Englewood Cliffs, New Jersey: Prentice Hall.

_____. 1975. "The Present Status of Structural-Functional Theory in Sociology." In Lewis A. Coser, (Ed.), *The idea of Social Structure: Papers in Honor of Robert K. Merton.* New York: Harcourt Brace Jovanovich.

Pearlin, Leonard I. and Melvin L. Kohn. 1966. "Social Class, Occupation, and Parental Values." *American Sociological Review*, 31: 466-479.

Peterson, Richard A. 1979. "Revitalizing the Culture Concept." In Alex Inkeles, James Coleman, Ralph H. Turner, (Eds.), *Annual Review of Sociology.* Volume 5. Palo Alto, California: Annual Reviews Inc., 137-166.

Pettigrew, Thomas F. 1964. *Profile of the Negro American*. Princeton: Van Nostrand.

Radcliffe-Brown. A. R. 1922. *The Andaman Islanders*. New York: Cambridge University Press.

_____. 1952. "On Social Structure." In A. R. Radcliffe-Brown, *Structure and Function in Primitive Society*. Glencoe, Illinois: The Free Press, 188-204.

Redfield, Robert. 1947. "The Folk Society." *American Journal of Sociology*, 52: 293-308.

_____.1957. *The Primitive World and Its Transformations*. Ithaca, New York: Cornell University Press.

Riesman, David. 1950. *The Lonely Crowd*. New Haven: Yale University Press.

Rogers, Carl R. 1951. *Client-Centered Therapy*. Boston: Houghton Mifflin Co.

Rokeach, Milton. 1973. *The Nature of Human Values*. New York: Free Press.

_____. 1979. *Understanding Human Values*. New York: The Free Press.

Rosenberg, B.G. 1971. "Roles and Social Control: Changing Concepts of Masculinity-Femininity." In John Paul Scott and Sarah F. Scott, (Eds.), *Social Control and Social Change*. Chicago: University of Chicago Press, 43-72.

Ross, Edward A. 1916. *Social Control*. New York: Macmillan. Originally Published in 1901.

_____. 1959. *Social Control and the Foundations of Sociology*, Edited by Edgar F. Borgatta and Henry J. Meyer. Boston: Beacon Press.

Rudoff, Alvin and George DeVos. 1970. "Subcultural Variations in the Perception of Parental Roles." San Jose, California: Unpublished manuscript.

Rushing, William A. 1969. "Role Conflict and Alcoholism." In William A. Rushing, (Ed.), *Deviant Behavior and Social Process*. Chicago: Rand McNally and Co., 292-300.

Rieff, Philip. 1975. "The Triumph of the Therapeutic." In F. James Davis and Richard Stivers, (Eds.), *The Collective Definition of Deviance*. New York: The Free Press, 392-410.

Runciman, W. G. 1970. *Sociology in Its Place and Other Essays.* London: Cambridge University Press.

Sagarin, Edward. 1975. *Deviants and Deviance.* New York: Praeger Publishers.

Sampson, Harold, Sheldon L. Messinger, and Robert D. Towne. 1962. "Family Processes and Becoming a Mental Patient." *American Journal of Sociology,* 68: 88-96.

Sapir, Edward. 1961. *Culture, Language and Personality.* Edited by David G. Mandelbaum. Berkeley: University of California Press.

Sarbin, Theodore R. 1954. "Role Theory." In Gardner Lindzey, (Ed.), *Handbook of Social Psychology.* Volume 1. Reading, Mass.: Addison-Wesley Publishing Co., Inc., 223-258.

Shaw, Clifford R. and Henry D. McKay. 1942. *Juvenile Delinquency and Urban Areas.* Chicago: University of Chicago Press.

Scheff, Thomas J. 1964. "The Societal Reaction to Deviance: Ascriptive Elements in the Psychiatric Screening of Mental Patients in a Midwestern State." *Social Problems,* 11: 401-413.

_____. 1966. *Being Mentally Ill.* Chicago: Aldine Publishing Co.

Schur, Edwin M. 1971. *Labeling Deviant Behavior: Its Sociological Implications.* New York: Harper & Row.

Schutz, Alfred. 1964. *Collected Papers.* The Hague: Martinus Nyhoff.

Scott, John Paul and Sarah F. Scott. 1971. (Eds.), *Social Control and Social Change.* Chicago: University of Chicago Press.

Sheldon, William H. 1942. *The Varieties of Temperament: A Psychology of Constitutional Differences.* New York: Harper & Brothers Publishing.

_____. 1949. *Varieties of Delinquent Youth: An Introduction to Constitutional Psychiatry.* New York: Harper & Row.

Shibutani, Tamotsu. 1961. *Society and Personality.* Englewood Cliffs, New Jersey: Prentice-Hall, Inc.

Shils, Edward A. 1970. "Deference." In Edward O. Laumann, Paul M. Siegel and Robert W. Hodge, (Eds.), *The Logic of Social Hierarchies.* Chicago: Markham Publishing Co., 420-448.

Short, James F. Jr. 1964. "Gang Delinquency and Anomie." In Marshall B. Clinard, (Ed.), *Anomie and Deviant Behavior.* New York: The Free Press, 198-127.

118

Sieber, Sam D. 1974. "Toward a Theory of Role Accumulation." *American Sociological Review*, 39: 567-578.

Simmons, J. L. 1969. *Deviants*. California: Glendessary Press.

Slomczynski, K.M., J. Miller, M.L. Kohm. 1981. "Stratification, Work and Values." *American Sociological Review*, 46: 720-744.

Small, Albion W. and George E. Vincent. 1894. *An Introduction to the Study of Society*. New York: American.

Smelser, Neil J. 1959. *Social Change in the Industrial Revolution*. Chicago: University of Chicago Press.

_____ and W. T. Smelser, (Eds.), 1963. *Personality and Social Systems*. New York: Wiley.

_____. 1967. *Sociology*. New York: Wiley & Sons, Inc.

Sofer, Elaine G. 1961. "Inner-Direction, Other Direction and Autonomy: A Study of College Students." In Seymour M. Lipset and Leo Lewenthal, (Eds.), *Culture and Social Character*. New York: The Free Press, 316-348.

Sorokin, Pitirim A. 1959. *Social and Cultural Mobility*. Glencoe Illinois: The Free Press.

Spates, James L. 1976. "Counterculture and Domiant Cultural Values." *American Sociological Review*, 41: 868-883.

_____. 1983. "The Sociology of Values." In Ralph Turner and James F. Short, Jr., (Eds.), *Annual Review of Sociology*. Volume 9. Palo Alto: Annual Reviews Inc., 27-49.

Spencer, Herbert. 1897. *Principles of Sociology*. New York; D. Appleton. Three volumes, volume 1, 439; volume 2, 24- 34, 220-226.

Spengler, Oswald. 1926-1928. *The Decline of the West*. Translated by Charles Francis Atkinson. New York: Alfred A. Knopf.

Stewart, Don and Thomas Hoult. 1960. "A Social-Psychological Theory of the Authoritarian Personality." *American Journal of Sociology*, 65: 274-279.

Stouffer, Samuel A. and Jackson Toby. 1951. "Role Conflict and Personality." *American Journal of Sociology*, 56: 395-406.

Sullivan, Harry S. 1953. *The Interpersonal Theory of Psychiatry*. New York: Norton.

Sumner, William G. 1906. *Folkways*. New York: Ginn. Reissued several times.

Sutherland, Edwin H. 1939. *Principles of Criminology*. Third edition. Chicago: J. B. Lippincott Co.

Sykes, Greshman and David Matza. 1957. "Techniques of Neutralization: A Theory of Delinquency." *American Sociological Review*, 22: 664-670.

Szasz, Thomas S. 1961. *The Myth of Mental Illness: Foundations of a Theory of Personal Conduct*. London: Secker & Warberg.

Tappan, Paul W. 1960. *Crime, Justice and Correction*. New York: McGraw-Hill Book Co., Inc.

Thoits, Peggy A. 1983. "Multiple Identities and Psychological Well-Being: A Reformulation and Test of the Social Isolation Hypothesis." *American Sociological Review*, 48: 174-187.

Thomas, W. I. and Florian Znaniecki. 1921. *The Polish Peasant In Europe and America*. Chicago: University of Chicago Press.

_____. 1927. *The Unadjusted Girl*. Boston: Little, Brown, and Co.

_____. 1928. *The Child in America: Behavior Problems and Programs*. New York: Alfred A. Knopf, Inc.

Thornberry, Terence P. and Margaret Farnworth. 1982. "Social Correlates of Criminal Involvement: Further Evidence on the Relationship Between Social Status and Criminal Behavior." *American Sociological Review*, 47: 505-518.

Tumin, Melvin M. 1967. *Social Stratification*. Enlewood Cliffs, New Jersey: Prentice-Hall, Inc.

Turner, Ralph H. 1968. "Role: Sociological Aspects." In D. Sills, (Ed.), *International Encyclopedia of the Social Sciences*. Volume 13. New York: The Free Press. 552-557.

_____. 1972. "Deviance Avowal as Neutralization of Committment." *Social Problems*, 19: 308-321.

Tylor, Sir Edward Burnett. 1958. *The Origins of Culture*. Part I: Of "Primitive Culture." New York: Harper Torchbooks.

Toby, Jackson. 1950. "Some Variables in Role-Conflicting Analysis." *Social Forces*, 30: 324-327.

Ullman, A. D. 1965. *Sociocultural Foundations of Personality*. Boston: Hougton Mifflin.

120

United Nations. 1952. *Comparative Surveys on Juvenile Delinquency*. Part II: Europe. New York: United Nations Department of Social Affairs, Division of Social Welfare.

Van Gennep, Arnold. 1960. *Rites of Passage*. Translated by M. K. Vizedom and G. L Caffee. Chicago: University of Chicago Press. Originally Published in 1908.

Vernon, Philip E. and Gordon W. Allport. 1931. "A Test For Personal Values." *Journal of Abnormal Social Psychology*, 26: 231-248.

Vold, George B. 1958. *Theoretical Criminology*. New York: Oxford University Press.

Waller, Willard. 1936. "Social Problems and the Mores." *American Sociological Review*, 1: 922-933.

Weber, Max. 1958. "Class, Status, Party." In H. H. Gerth and C. Wright Mills. From Max Weber: *Essays in Sociology*. New York: Oxford University Press.

Wiley, Norbert F. 1967. "The Ethnic Mobility Trap and Stratification Theory." *Social Problems*, 15: 147-159.

Williams, Robin M. Jr. 1970. *American Society: A Sociological Interpratation.* Third Edition. New York: Knopf.

Williams, R. 1976. "Developments in the Sociology of Culture." *Sociology*, 10.

Wolff, Kurt H. 1950. *The Sociology of Georg Simmel*. Glencoe, Illinois: The Free Press.

Wright, James D. and Sonia R. Wright. 1976. "Social Class and Parental Values for Children: A Partial Replication and Extension of the Kohn Thesis." *American Sociological Review*, 41: 527-537.

Wrong, Dennis. 1961. "The Oversocialized Conception of Man in Modern Sociology." *American Sociological Review*, 26: 183-193.

Yinger, Milton J. 1965. *Toward a Field Theory of Behavior*. New York: McGraw-Hill Book Co.

Yochelson, Samuel and Stanton E. Samenow. 1976. *The Criminal Personality. Volume I: Profile For Change*. New York: Jason Aronson.

Zaleznik, A., C. R. Christenson, and F. J. Roethlisberger, in Collaboration with George C. Homans. 1958. *The Motivation, Productivity, and Satisfaction of Workers*. Cambridge: Harvard University Press.

Znaniecki, Florian. 1949. "Social Groups as Products of Participating Individuals." *American Journal of Sociology*, 44: 799-811.

_____. 1965. *Social Relations and Social Roles*. San Francisco: Chandler Publishing Co., Chapter 10.

INDEX